Dramas of Kalalau

TERENCE JAMES MOELLER

WITH WILLIAM GLADSTONE

EDITED BY CHRIS COOK

MUTUAL PUBLISHING

This book is dedicated to my three children,
Aaron, Jonathan, and Noelani Moeller.

Disclaimer:
The author and publisher of Dramas of Kalalau disclaim any responsibility for any and all injuries that readers of this book may incur while exploring the Nā Pali Trail and Kalalau Valley. There are numerous natural hazards in this remote terrain and anyone entering therein does so at their own risk.

Library of Congress Cataloging-in-Publication Data

Dramas of Kalalau / by Terence James Moeller
      p. cm.
  Anthology of writings, interviews, and historical fiction about Kalalau Valley on the island of Kauai.
  Includes bibliographical references.
  ISBN 1-56647-827-8 (softcover : alk. paper)
  1. Kauai (Hawaii)--Literary collections. 2. American literature--Hawaii--Kauai. I. Moeller, Terence James.
PS571.H3D73 2007
810.8'0996941--dc22
                                        2006039477

ISBN-10: 1-56647-827-8
ISBN-13: 978-1-56647-827-4

First Printing, October 2007
1 2 3 4 5 6 7 8 9

Mutual Publishing, LLC
1215 Center Street, Suite 210
Honolulu, Hawai'i 96816
Ph: 808-732-1709 / Fax: 808-734-4094
email: info@mutualpublishing.com
www.mutualpublishing.com

Printed in China

Contents

PREFACE

Dramas of Kalalau is the brainchild of Bill Gladstone, president of Waterside Productions, who was introduced to Kalalau by his friend and guide Ikaika Pratt of Kaua'i. As he experienced the Hawaiian way of living off the land in Kalalau, Bill became fascinated with the secret society that lived within the valley. Listening to ancient tales and modern day dramas around a campfire, the concept of collecting these stories in a book emerged. The idea took on a life of its own and developed over a period of seven years and as many expeditions into Kalalau.

Trail guide Ikaika brings a unique perspective to the story of Kalalau. He is a native Hawaiian naturalist with thirty-eight years of experience of going into Kalalau. I am a Kaua'i-based independent producer whose only previous experience in Kalalau was when I was marooned there in the 1970s. With the help of 'ohana, we've assembled a unique collection of Kalalau's history, contemporary human drama, humor, poetry, and practical advice for those venturing in.

In an effort to capture the "Kalalau experience," I made several solo hikes into the valley, each time returning with a more profound interest in Nā Pali and its place in Hawaiian lore. It soon became apparent that years of intensive research would be necessary to tell the whole story of Kalalau with its myriad legends, traditions, and myths. Any errors of fact, translation, interpretation, omission, and lapses in style and memory are the sole responsibility of this writer, who regards himself more of a humorist than historian.

I wrote the stories collected in the main section of the book as I heard them while attempting to place them within some historical context. This was accomplished with the aid of an expert native Hawaiian trail guide, a pocket tape recorder, and the many unforgettable characters that I met along the way.

The book provides a valley-by-valley description of the hike along the Kalalau Trail, an insiders' view of Kalalau, and a collection of modern first-person accounts emanating out of the valley. Some of these were obtained through correspondence with former residents of Kalalau, some were discovered in the archives of the *Garden Island* newspaper, but most were a matter of being at the right place at the right time. These tales represent only a fraction of those that may exist, yet capture the spirit of Kalalau, providing a rare glimpse into a world that few people ever experience.

ACKNOWLEDGMENTS

I gratefully acknowledge the valuable assistance of the following in creating *Dramas of Kalalau*:

William F. Gladstone—president/founder of Waterside Productions, Inc. whose forbearance opened the way for this book to be written; Bennett Hymer of Mutual Publishing for the honor of being represented by the best in Hawai'i; Lloyd Imuaikaika Pratt—my trail guide whose indefatigable energy and optimism made Kalalau an unforgettable experience; Frances Fraizer—a renowned Kaua'i historian who was kind enough to do a phone interview with me concerning the life and times of Ko'olau; W.S. Merwin—author of *The Folding Cliffs*, a 300-page epic poem about Kalalau, referenced herein; the publisher and editor of the *Garden Island* newspaper— for providing use of stories about Kalalau discovered in the archives; Kona Lowell—a highly gifted poet who contributed to this book; Frederick B. Wichman—author of *Kaua'i: Ancient Place-Names and Their Stories*; short story contributors Bobo, Dr. Gary Saldana, Sky, and Tom Williams; and most importantly Claudia Dawn Moeller—my lovely wife who was the one who suffered most from my writer's block, and is the guardian of my solitude and the inspiration for every romantic impulse.

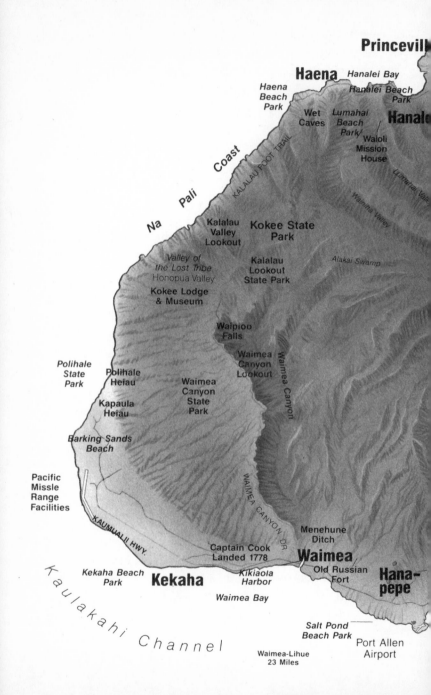

Destination Kalalau

All their high sayings returned to sand and each of them had once faced the rain and wind the sun and the night sky with bare rock and the shining black drapery and jagged stone salients of lava and across them the weather had broken measureless all through time before time and before the first waifs of life had found their way to those surfaces solitary travelers lifted by storms and long swells to a naked place where one day they found company.

—The Folding Cliffs, W.S. Merwin

Destination Kalalau

We met at Kēʻē Beach in Hāʻena. For tourists traveling west on Kūhiō Highway it is the end of the line. But for Ikaika and me, whose destination is Kalalau Valley, it is the beginning. For the next seven hours we will be hiking one of the most breathtakingly beautiful trails on earth; a place where myth, legend, and modern-day dramas merge.

Kēʻē Beach is rich in native Hawaiian sites, and the fringing reefs and abundance of freshwater streams in the area provided an ideal setting for Kauaʻi's first Polynesian settlers, who arrived over a millennium ago.

Native Hawaiian villages dotted Nā Pali from the Kēʻē area to Miloliʻi Valley on the west end of Nā Pali until about 1920. The series of villages, with Kalalau being the main one, made up the most isolated inhabited area in all the Hawaiian Islands, according to E.S. Craighall Handy in his definitive study of native Hawaiian agriculture, *Native Planters in Old Hawaii*. This isolation gave Kalalau a notorious reference in Hawaiian proverbs. The name came to mean wandering aimlessly, or to go astray. In the old days when a person had gone off the deep end, locals might say, "He had gone to Kalalau."

The spectacular beauty of Nā Pali served as a fitting backdrop to some of the most unique cultural practices of old Hawaiʻi.

The peak behind the trailhead that leads into Nā Pali located just mauka of the parking lot at Kēʻē is a mountain known to Hawaiians as Makana, or the gift. The Hawaiians have a saying, E uhi ana ka wa i hala i na mea i hala (passing time obscures the past), and the place name for Makana is a prime example of this. The peak is rated as the second most recognizable landmark in Hawai'i, after O'ahu's Diamond Head. This renown for the dramatic outline of Makana's east face began when the peak was featured as a backdrop to the mysterious island of Bali Hai in the 1957 Hollywood musical *South Pacific*. Tour guides then began referring to Makana as Bali Hai, obscuring the peak's real name. Today most visitors, and many Kaua'i residents, know Makana only as Bali Hai.

Kama'āina Kaua'i place-name collector and author Frederick Wichman of Hā'ena provides an accurate account of Makana's name in his book *Kaua'i: Ancient Place-Names and Their Stories*. Without Wichman's years of research into Kaua'i's ancient place names, the heritage of many of the locations mentioned herein would have been forgotten.

Hawaiians named each peak, reef, trail, beach, valley, and stream along Nā Pali. Some place names provided warnings about dangerous coastal conditions; others marked the location of an historic event or chapter in a Hawaiian legend. Most had several levels of meaning which included the literal one, as well as those that held a spiritual or sexual connotation. Some of the place names live on in Hawaiian song and hula.

Makana stands as a symbol of the beauty of Nā Pali. Silhouetted against the setting sun, this majestic point can be seen on the North Shore from as far away as Kīlauea. A short hike along a lava rock trail following the perimeter of Kē'ē beach leads to the base of Makana and the site of the foremost ancient hula halau (school) in the Hawaiian Islands, known as Ke-ahu-a-Laka.

Hula students gathered here from across Kaua'i and from other islands to spend years in intense hula study. After memorizing hundreds of chants and expertly performing a variety of hula styles, the student had to pass one final test in order to graduate—a swim from Kē'ē Beach west along its rapidly outflowing channel to Nahiki, a picturesque lava-rock-walled bay located over a hundred feet below the halau. If they made it without being devoured by the sharks [who, according to legend, were "fed by the chiefess"], they were awarded the title kumu hula, or master hula instructor.

A cliff high up on the face of Makana, as well as a cliff known as Kamaile that towers over Nu'alolo Kai about twelve miles to the west, was renowned throughout Hawai'i for the throwing of Nā Pali 'Ōahi o Makana, a unique Hawaiian-style fireworks display. The masters of this art waited for just the right trade wind conditions to hold the event. They would carry a fresh supply of long softwood hau and pāpala sticks some 1,600 feet up to a platform carved out of the cliff side where another stack of wood brought up during a previous 'ōahi, had been sufficiently dried and was ready to be used. People from all over the island gathered at a sandy open space near Kē'ē for three days of feasts, songs, and dance culminating in the spectacular fire-throwing event. The long shafts resembled missiles as the hollowed firebrands sailed hundreds of yards offshore, leaving a spectacular trail of burning embers in their wake. Some spectators watched offshore in outrigger canoes. Others gathered the still-smoldering sticks and burnt themselves on the chest as a souvenir to prove they had seen in person the 'ōahi.

A comparison of the 'ōahi tradition of Makana with the tourist's vision of Bali Hai represents an important element of this book. That is, preserving not only aspects of the little-known ancient Hawaiian era at Kalalau, but also a record of its modern era, which in many respects has been equally obscured.

The roots of the *Dramas of Kalalau* stretch back in time to the first settlers of Nā Pali. Though Kaua'i is said to be the first inhabited Hawaiian Island, there is no consensus on where the first arriving seafaring canoes landed on Nā Pali. Some clues came from an archaeological dig led by Kenneth Emory of the Bishop Museum in the late 1950s and early 1960s of a fishing village at Nu'alolo Kai that unearthed over four hundred Nā Pali artifacts. However, Emory's work just scratched the surface, for it would take an archaeologist a lifetime to uncover the walls and terraces that are visible from the Kalalau Trail alone.

Early historical Nā Pali accounts include the journal of a double-hulled canoe voyage down Nā Pali made by Congregational missionary Hiram Bingham in 1821, and a one-day canoe trip by a Honolulu judge made in the 1840s. Captain James Cook, who discovered the Hawaiian Islands in 1778, never sailed along Nā Pali, though two of his officers would be the first to record a passage along Nā Pali. George Dixon, captain of the *Queen Charlotte*, wrote of Nā Pali in his journals published in 1789, saying the coast seemed uninhabited. Lt. George Vancouver returned in 1794 and made the passage.

These Western accounts provide a brief glimpse into the secrets of Nā Pali's past. Chants passed down orally from generation to generation, and myths and legends told through hula, are the only nonarchaeological native Hawaiian records of Nā Pali's ancient past.

Scholars, mainstream writers, and native Hawaiians give the early Polynesian inhabitants of Nā Pali a variety of names. Some call them kanaka maoli. Others simply call them Hawaiians or Tahitians. Many researchers concur that the legendary Menehune were the first, but their influence was later eclipsed by the arrival of other more dominant immigrants from the South Pacific. Perhaps a new name distinct from other Polynesian settlers is needed, like Proto-Nā Palian. Whatever one chooses to call them, it is certain that these first settlers migrated to Hawai'i hundreds of years before the first European explorers of the sixteenth century ever set sail in the Pacific.

Native plants and animals are somewhat limited along the Kalalau Trail. Most of the notable and rare native honeycreeper forest birds live high above the coast in the Kōke'e-Alaka'i Swamp area. The forest birds along the trail are mainly introduced varieties, though you may see native sea birds soaring offshore, like the Laysan albatross or the frigate bird, known in Hawai'i as the 'iwa.

Botanists from the National Tropical Botanical Garden have found previously undiscovered species of orchids and other plants deep in the valleys of Nā Pali. Along the wetter sections of the trail around Hanakāpī'ai the rare saintjobnianus hibiscus with tangerine colored blossoms is sometimes spotted. This plant is endemic and indigenous to Nā Pali. Native marine life is often seen offshore, with humpback whales arriving in winter, green sea turtles munching on coastal limu (seaweed) year-round, and spinner dolphins escorting tour boats along the coast.

Underlying life on Nā Pali is its geological past. The island's main mass was several thousand feet higher than it is today. Along this volcanic dome's north side secondary massive lava eruptions formed sections of Nā Pali and the Hanalei side of the North Shore. Wind, rains, and huge winter waves carved the coastline, fluting the cliffs that give Kalalau its place name of kala, or fluted, lau (leaves). State of art underwater scanning technology is giving geologists a clearer picture of how the cliffs, valleys, and shoreline of Nā Pali were formed. In the late 1980s the remains of huge landslides were found stretching out for miles at the bottom of the Pacific in waters off Nā Pali. This clearly demonstrated that hundreds of yards of the coastline collapsed and fell into the sea, helping to give the coast its distinctive look. The erosion may one day in the future open up Waimea Canyon on the Westside of Kaua'i to Kalalau Valley, for the narrow plateau four thousand feet above Kalalau Valley is slowly eroding.

The highest peaks looming mauka of the Kalalau Trail are Waiahuakua above Pōhakuao Valley at 3,320 feet; Alealau, at 3,875 feet, which the Ka'a'alahina Ridge on the east end of Kalalau Valley leads up to; Pihea at 4,284 feet behind Kalalau Valley; and Kalahu, the peak between Kalalau and Honopū Valley, at 3,682 feet.

The Kalalau Trail

The Kalalau Trail crosses eleven miles of some of the most rugged coastal terrain in Hawai'i, running from the trailhead at Kē'ē Beach to Kalalau Beach.

The long, arduous hike is worth it, for anyone making it on foot to Kalalau and back can expect to experience an unforgettable journey.

For a preview of the trail, walk back toward Hanalei along the beach at Kē'ē for about one hundred yards. This provides a quick look at what's ahead, with an excellent overview of the coast from Kē'ē to Kalalau to Alapa'i Point at Nu'alolo.

Experienced hikers can complete the trail from Kē'ē to Kalalau in five to seven hours, depending on how dry the weather conditions have been. Strong hikers who know the trail can begin in the morning and finish well before dusk. But that's going all out. Many hikers choose to break up the journey into two days, stopping past the halfway mark at the State Parks' campsite at Hanakoa Valley.

Most of the travelers you see starting out on the trail at Kē'ē are day hikers, and take a relatively quick, two-miles jaunt to Hanakāpī'ai, the first major valley along the trail.

The road to the trailhead is known as the Kūhiō Highway, which meanders along the coast from the North Shore, through Hanalei town, past the Wainiha Store and the Limahuli National Botanical Garden to Kē'ē Beach in Hā'ena where the road ends. A small wooden shelter that contains a display of trail information and maps marks the beginning of the trail. Wry notes and comments from hikers who've returned from Kalalau are often posted here and are worth reading for a realistic assessment of what lies ahead on the trail.

It's not advisable to leave a vehicle in the crowded parking area at Kē'ē Beach. If you are planning to stay overnight or longer, try to arrange to be dropped off at Kē'ē. Ideally the best time to leave is about 5:00 a.m. so that when you face the steepest part of the trail, just past Hanakāpī'ai, the sun is just coming up.

The Kalalau Trail isn't a place to push your physical capabilities beyond a reasonable limit, a practice that has placed many Kaua'i visitors in danger. There are no emergency services available within Nā Pali. If you are incapacitated, someone must hike out to alert rescuers or signal to a passing tour boat or helicopter to send help. The time between finding help and a rescue can be considerable. Cell phone signals are non-existent in Nā Pali. The cost of a Nā Pali rescue is expensive and may be passed on to the victims. Members of the Kaua'i Fire Department and Kaua'i lifeguards from the North Shore are routinely involved in rescues of stranded hikers and kayakers along the coast. Most of the time these situations can be avoided simply by being prepared and making safety the first priority on the trail.

Visitors are strongly advised to abide by state and county camping regulations for their own safety and well-being as well as the preservation of the delicate ecosystems along Nā Pali.

In accordance with the state Department of Land and Natural Resources' rules, you must obtain a camping permit in advance to stay in the Nā Pali Coast State Park. The cost is $10 per person per night. You can obtain a permit at the State Parks office in the Līhu'e state building on Umi Street, or at the State Parks office in Honolulu. Officially, day-use permits are also required if you hike beyond Hanakāpī'ai, even if you return to Kē'ē the same day.

Camping permits are limited to five consecutive nights, with no two consecutive nights allowed at the campsites at Hanakāpī'ai or Hanakoa valleys.

The state's campsites are somewhat primitive and lack sources of safe drinking water. There are toilets at the three campsites along the way, but they are often found to be less than sanitary.

Three essentials for all hikers heading into Kalalau are proper footwear, a comfortable pack, and plenty of drinking water.

One Hawaiian, fresh off the trail, joked that hikers wearing tennis shoes on the Nā Pali "might as well throw themselves over the cliffs at the beginning." Lightweight hiking shoes with good traction are essential. Most hikers use a staff to support themselves along the trail, and staffs can be found left behind at the head of the trail. If you are going all the way to Kalalau, it is wise to choose a light staff that provides good balance, though it can be a burden to carry on those long, uphill switchbacks ahead.

It's inadvisable to drink from streams on the way to Kalalau due to the dangers of leptospirosis (a liver fluke infestation that has claimed several lives on Kaua'i) in the freshwater, thus the need to carry in a good supply of drinking water for the hours on the trail. Once at your campsite, water purification tablets or a water filter are needed to purify stream water.

Traveling as light as possible is advisable. However, to camp comfortably you should pack a lightweight sleeping bag, a sleeping pad, a tent or tarp, a first-aid kit, insect repellent, sunscreen, rain gear, and soap that is biodegradable.

A journey along the Kalalau Trail can be broken down into three distinct passages. A warm-up of one mile up and then one mile down to the stream and beach at Hanakāpī'ai Valley. Then a rigorous, switchbacking four-mile trek through a lowland forest in and out of the narrow hanging valleys of Ho'olulu and Waiahuakua to a rest area at Hanakoa Valley. The final leg is the longest, the most dangerous, but also the most scenic. Along the five-mile stretch from Hanakoa to the beach at Kalalau the coastline opens up and the climate is drier. Cut into cliffsides hundreds of feet above the Pacific, sections of the trail here are the most daunting, with the potential for a fall, especially in wet and muddy conditions.

The reality of hiking the Kalalau Trail begins to set in within the first ten feet as you head up a stone path laid in the 1930s. Any illusion that the journey is going to be a leisurely "walk in the park" quickly fades as the path heads straight uphill.

One tourist wrote: "My initial thought upon viewing the trail was, this is going to be tough. After my first step we were climbing over huge rocks and old stems. The trails were steep and narrow." Another wrote, "Some portions of the trail don't deserve the dignity of that title."

This may seem a bit hyperbolic, but the trail is tougher than travel writers usually portray it. Several of the dramas recorded in this book occurred because hikers went in, unaware of their surroundings and their own physical limitations.

Hiking into Kalalau with an experienced trail guide is recommended for malihini (newcomers).

Ikaika has guided everyone from school children to the elderly into Kalalau and believes that most people can make the eleven-mile hike if the conditions are right.

At the trailhead we fortunately met Bobo, a Hanalei woman formerly known as the Calamity Jane of Kalalau. Her exploits in Kalalau are legendary. Now in middle age, she is still occasionally spotted on the trail at the lookouts with her long, beautiful, gray hair flying in the breeze. She was planning to hike to Hanakāpīʻai to do some bodysurfing on the day of the first big winter swell. Bobo told us that she "just had to be there."

Along the trail I tape-recorded an interview with this incredibly resilient grandmother. She reminisced about her "outlaw days" living in the valley. At the pace Bobo set, it was difficult at times to keep my mike in range, but her amazing stories were well worth the effort.

"Whenever I would leave Kalalau," she said, "it was like a cowboy coming in off the range. I would spend all my pakalolo (marijuana) money and just go wild. Then, after I had been let out of jail, or the hospital, I would swim back to the valley with my tail between my legs. Man that stuff takes its toll on you."

There were once distance markers posted by the state forest service every half mile or so, but they are no longer maintained and are seldom spotted past Hanakoa Valley.

The first mile on the way to Hanakāpīʻai is a steady climb, while the second mile is a descent to the pocket beach.

We rested at the half-mile mark, which at four hundred feet above sea level offers an excellent view of Kēʻē Beach behind and a look ahead at the incredibly scenic towering peaks and coastal valleys of Nā Pali ten miles down the coast. The contrast of the landscape's color is vivid here. The verdant valleys at the Hāʻena end of the trail (where it rains seventy-five inches a year) gradually give way to the red-dirt ridges near Kalalau on the noticeably drier Leeward side of Nā Pali.

From the half-mile point one can see the privately owned island of Niʻihau across the Kaulakahi Channel. There used to be a great deal of interaction between the people of Kalalau Valley and the isolated island of Niʻihau, located seventeen miles off Kauaʻi's Westside. Many Hawaiian families living on Kauaʻi's North Shore today trace their roots to both places. As Kauaʻi modernized in the mid-1800s with the founding of sugar cane plantations along the coast from Hanalei to Kekaha their ancestors gradually moved out of Nā Pali.

Sections of an ancient trail used by native Hawaiians for hundreds of years were expanded in the mid-1800s for commercial reasons. Gottfried Wundenberg, a German immigrant to Hawaiʻi and the Hawaiian Kingdom's Controller of Roads for Kauaʻi at the time, set off over four hundred dynamite blasts along the trail in 1860. The work was done to allow room for donkeys to haul out coffee, oranges, and other agricultural products grown in Nā Pali. Hanakāpīʻai Valley was once planted in coffee, and the ruins of a small mill and valley cabin constructed by the Deverill family of Hanalei, who planted the trees, are still visible.

As you approach a small brook at the mile-and-a-half marker you pass under a natural arbor of liliko'i (passion fruit). This nonnative plant is a good example of the changes Nā Pali has undergone since the arrival of Polynesians and Westerners. Where landscapes made up of totally native plants once existed, plants brought from the South Pacific, Asia, and the Americas now thrive. Picturesque hala trees, another introduced Polynesian plant, frame the first view of Hanakāpī'ai Beach. Its leaves, known as lau hala, were used by native Hawaiians to weave mats and sails.

From here the trail makes an equally steady descent to Hanakāpī'ai Stream where it meets the ocean. Hanakāpī'ai is the only place where the trail reaches sea level until it ends at Kalalau Beach.

Periodically ropes are strung across the stream, but they are discouraged by park rangers because hikers are tempted to use them in dangerous flood conditions and run the risk of being swept out to sea. If the water level of a stream is above your knees, beware of crossing a stream on Nā Pali. Flood conditions may recede as quickly as they rise, letting you safely proceed.

When a flash flood hits, often before you see it, you will hear the boulders crashing underwater as they are moved downstream. That's the time to start looking for high ground. These streams are extremely narrow with a steep incline. In a rain forest the water level can rise radically in moments. The best thing to do in this situation is to be patient and stay clear of the stream until the flood passes. Between the people being swept away in the stream, caught in a heavy riptide, or trapped in the sea caves, Hanakāpī'ai keeps the Kaua'i rescue teams quite busy.

Wading or swimming in the shorebreak at Hanakāpī'ai in winter is a dangerous practice. A warning sign with over forty tally marks on it indicates the number of drownings there. Surf and currents can be dangerous along Nā Pali, even in the calm water months of summer for there are no fringing reefs to provide protection from open-ocean conditions. There are no lifeguards on Nā Pali, and only swimmers or surfers experienced with local conditions should venture far from shore.

A side-trip for hikers is a two-mile round-trip mauka walk to Hanakāpī'ai Falls. The trail, which cuts across Hanakāpī'ai Stream several times, was partly destroyed by the hurricanes that hit Kaua'i in 1982 and 1992. Rainwater originating in the Alaka'i Swamp some four thousand feet above cascades down the 120-foot waterfall. Beware of standing directly beneath the falls, for loose lava rocks often fall down with the streamwater.

The steep climb beyond the rest stop at Hanakāpī'ai Stream takes you through fourteen switchbacks on the way up the western ridge of the valley, well past the day hikers who rarely go beyond this point. As you approach the top of the ridge a stand of hundreds of sisal plants, with shafts twenty to thirty feet tall, eclipse the reverse view of Hanakāpī'ai Beach. Sisal is another commercially introduced plant, once used to replace hemp in nineteenth-century rope making for sailing ships.

The two-and-a-half-mile mark offers a beautiful view back to Kē'ē. As you pass over parts of the trail that have water trickling off the rocks, notice the delicate maiden-hair fern growing underneath. It is used to weave the haku (lei)—a beautiful, flowered wreath worn on the head.

The three-and-one-quarter mile marker is the highest point on the entire trail at about eight hundred feet above sea level. Hikers, beginning to feel the strain of the trail, often refresh themselves here at the giant boulder known as "space rock." There is a natural-chair dip in the rock; for a thrill, sit down, lean forward, and look down to see the ocean eight hundred feet directly below. This monolith cut into the face of the sea cliffs is a highly visible landmark from the sea.

You enter Ho'olulu Valley at the three-and-a-half mile marker. This area, like most of the valleys on the way to Kalalau, was once planted extensively in taro. The stone terraces that are common along the entire Nā Pali coast are clearly visible from the trail there. From December to May humpback whales are seen from this point, breaching a few hundred yards offshore.

Beyond this point the trail crosses through Ho'olulu and into Waiahuakua Valley. The valleys encompass the State of Hawai'i's Hono o Nā Pali lowland forest. Camping is absolutely kapu (forbidden) in this protected ecological reserve.

The steadily declining trail has several cut-backs which lead into the picturesque Ho'olulu Valley. Right before the four-and-a-half-mile marker the first view opens up of Waiahuakua, a hanging valley best known for its landmark sea cave. Through the ages the Waiahuakua Stream eroded a hole through the top of the cave, allowing a cascading waterfall to pour straight into the Pacific. On calm days kayakers on their way to Kalalau paddle through the cave to refresh themselves under the falls. There are no house sites here, for the valley is believed to have been used solely for growing taro during the centuries when native Hawaiians populated Nā Pali. The trail on the western slope of Waiahuakua drops to the 400-foot level—its lowest point since the rise out of Hanakāpī'ai Valley. It continues to hug the coast until you enter Hanakoa Valley, the next major ahupua'a, at six miles. Here the temperature becomes noticeably cooler as you follow the contour of the valley mauka into Hanakoa at five hundred feet above sea level. Orange trees planted in the 1800s are abundant here, so you may want to pick a few to nourish yourself while hiking the arid, unshaded sections of the trail that lie ahead.

Past Hanakoa the climate becomes noticeably more Leeward than Windward, more barren with the lush rain forest environment giving way to sunny red-dirt landscapes.

An 1835 missionary census counted fifty native Hawaiians living in Hanakoa Valley, which was pre-dominantly rock-terraced taro patch land. Wild coffee plants today blanket the terraced walls and the rock-lined house sites located deeper in the valley.

At Hanakoa, State Parks maintain shelters on both sides of the Hanakoa Stream. Hikers and hunters share them. One may hear gunshots fired at wild goats by hunters from this point on, especially on weekends during hunting season. About a mile up the Hanakoa Stream is a beautiful waterfall, but if your destination at the end of the day is Kalalau, it is advisable to save that trip for a time when you plan to camp at Hanakoa.

During the rainy season, hikers should avoid wading out to the large boulders situated in the middle of the Hanakoa Stream. If the stream rises quickly, you may find yourself stranded. Less-experienced hikers attempt to forge the Hanakoa Stream when the current is too swift, and are often swept off their feet into the torrent. Getting in trouble here is more serious than in Hanakāpī'ai Valley, for it is extremely isolated—beyond the halfway point on the trail, and nearly a quarter-mile inland. Play it safe: In Hanakoa you are on your own.

Hanakoa translates as Bay of Koa trees or Bay of Warriors. According to Kaua'i legend collector Wichman, it was named after the Menehune chiefess Hanakeao. Like legendary Chiefess Hanakāpī'ai, Hanakeao too is said to have been with child when she slipped on the trail and fell to her death.

From Hanakoa Stream a gradual rise in the trail takes you to Manono Ridge and the seven-mile marker, which serves as a break for those making the hard, one-day trek from Kē'ē to Kalalau. An excellent view of the coast can be seen from an overlook here.

Pōhakuao (swimming rock) is the next ahupua'a on the trail, the last before entering Kalalau Valley. The geographical contrasts and wealth of legends attached to it make Pōhakuao an interesting last stop.

The valley is the smallest, yet coast-to-mountain the longest on Nā Pali. Pōhakuao also lies in the shadow of Alealau, at feet the highest pinnacle of all of the vertical cliffs of Nā

Pali, standing almost three times as tall as New York's former World Trade Center.

In a sea cave 300 feet below the trail is a rock named Pohaku Ku Mano or rock resembling shark. This natural formation, seventy-five feet long, has its tail in Hanakoa and its head, constantly showered by a waterfall, in Pōhakuao.

Another interesting feature as you pass the first of several gulches that make up Pōhakuao, is a handcrafted rock wall that borders the trail. Notice how each individual stone in the wall is naturally fitted. This is a prime example of the vast network of the ancient native Hawaiian-made walls and terraces erected over centuries throughout Nā Pali valleys.

Crossing Pōhakuao tests even veteran hikers. The path becomes steeper and barren culminating at the toughest twenty feet of the Kalalau Trail—the infamous Crawler's Ledge. Hikers anticipating the legendary narrow passes and steep cliffs along Nā Pali are not disappointed at Pōhakuao. Under normal conditions the seven-mile mark here is daunting, but manageable; in wet, stormy conditions, most often in winter, the gravelly soil at Pōhakuao becomes extremely unstable. Some navigate this series of switchbacks on their belly even before reaching the notorious Crawler's Ledge, which looms ahead.

Many hikers find this the most exhilarating passage on the Kalalau Trail. Some face their moment of truth at Crawler's Ledge, seriously considering turning around to face an even longer hike back to where they started. This is a tough decision because they are only two miles from the entrance to Kalalau Valley. Fireside tales of death-defying experiences here are not uncommon, though often exaggerated.

A fellow traveler from Japan, Yansu Ouyang, recalls his first experience along this pass: "We literally had to duck down and lean against the mountain to keep moving. The wind was so strong we were being hit by rocks and sand, which made it painful and difficult to move forward. Many times I wanted to turn around. Bad thoughts came through my head—getting knocked off the cliffs, dying, stuck in the middle with nowhere to turn. The trails became narrower and narrower after that. I was no longer able to walk facing forward. I had to face the mountain with my back toward the ocean grabbing on to whatever I could. I dug my finger into the dirt, and prayed that there was enough to keep me stable until the trail became visible again. Twenty minutes felt like a lifetime. We were not looking forward to passing that seventh-mile death path again on the way back. We tried not to think about it. Once we got to the point where we could see the death ledge, we stopped for twenty minutes, sat, ate snacks, and watched others. One couple turned around, afraid to keep going. That's when we braced ourselves for the worst."

Ikaika mentioned the time he came across a man literally crawling over Crawler's Ledge. He asked him, "Are you sick?" The man replied, "No, I'm scared of heights. I cannot take this trail any more." Ikaika knew he couldn't just leave him there, so he helped him to his feet and told him: "You hold on to one end of this stick, and I will be holding on to the other end. I want you to only look at the trail, or me, but do not look down. Trust me. I will walk you all the way."

Once they passed Pōhakuao, he was fine.

The author's son, Aaron Moeller, recalls the time that he was caught in a torrential rainstorm at night in Pōhakuao and nearly struck by a falling two-ton boulder in a landslide.

Emily, a trail veteran (known affectionately in Kalalau as Melinda's Mom), described her last experience hiking Crawler's Ledge. "Totally, totally frightening. I totally lost it the last time I came into Kalalau. It was pouring rain and I crawled across those switchbacks at the seven-mile mark with my fingers clinging to the mud."

Another female traveler put it most poetically: "The Nā Pali will bring out the fear of heights in the most confident and well-balanced soul."

The most remarkable thing is that regardless of how difficult this section was, or how terrified travelers may have been at the time, the majority of them would return to it in a heartbeat.

At Pōhakuao the mood of the trail seems to change with the seasons.

It is an awesome experience to walk along Pōhakuao in winter hearing the crash of the waves and feeling their vibrations against the sea cliffs, followed by a cool sea spray rising from 300 feet below.

At the foot of Pōhakuao Valley is the waterfall Kawaikuauhoealawaiʻa (water of the paddle handle of the fisherman). Today fishermen stop there when the surf is low in summer to cool off on their way down Nā Pali by pulling their boats under the cascading falls. Kamehameha, the warrior king from the Big Island of Hawaiʻi, never conquered Kauaʻi militarily. Nor did he "drink from Kawaikuauhoealawaiʻa Falls" as he once boasted that he would do. As fate would have it, on his way from Oʻahu to Kauaʻi canoes carrying his armies were destroyed during a storm at sea, never to return to the Garden Island.

At the eight-mile mark there is a flat, grassy camping area along the bluffs with a spectacular view of Kalalau and the surrounding coast. From that point one can see the broad, coastal plain at the base of Red Hill in the distance where many of the old Kalalau settlements once stood.

After hours on the trail, finally seeing Kalalau Valley within easy hiking range is an emotional charge. Thoughts of obstacles overcome along the way and the memory of the sheer pain of the journey are overshadowed by the sight of the mystical beauty of Kalalau shining in the distance like an emerald set upon a silver band.

Inside Kalalau Valley

Kalalau Valley evades description. Our trail guide, who has lived on every one of the islands, sees Kalalau as by far the most beautiful place in all of Hawai'i. Science fiction author Kathleen Goonan described Kalalau in *The Washington Post* as: "Being in Kalalau is like being given permission to see and touch the most intimate parts of the earth...even when you are awake it seems like you must be dreaming."

After facing the extremes of heat, rain, and fatigue, and finally the exhilaration of hiking nine-plus miles along the Kalalau Trail, you descend the red-dirt eastern boundary of the valley, a place simply known as Red Hill. Making it to Kalalau from Kē'ē on foot is an accomplishment shared only by those who are willing to endure the trail—a Nā Pali rite of initiation.

From the top of Red Hill, Ikaika gazed upon Kalalau Beach and the fringing reef at Nu'alolo Kai shining in the afternoon sun several miles down the coast.

"Home at last," he sighed.

The path down Red Hill to Kalalau Beach is steep and the soil is extremely unstable, so take your time. Blue Kalalau clay mixed in the red soil is a notable natural phenomenon. The trail forks off into mini-paths on the way down, but all converge at the bottom.

Visible on a flat plain at the base of Red Hill is a site dense in overgrown rock walls that once served as taro terraces and house sites. Here a large community of native Hawaiians resided for hundreds of years.

At the base of Ka'a'alaahina Ridge the trail forks left into a stand of guava and java plum trees.

Before long the dusty trail takes a small dip, and the Kalalau Stream appears like a virtual oasis. The senses are immediately quickened as a cool, fragrant breeze carries across the trail from the pali, filtering through the dry air.

Ikaika and JaNee's camp is located down a short path where the main trail meets the stream. The couple cleared away wild shrub that once surrounded the entire area restoring it with native plants and trees. To supplement their food supplies they cleared the area of boulders and planted a garden of local herbs, vegetables, and spices.

The first order of business after a seven-hour hike is to wash the trail off. A freshwater pool with a gorgeous ocean view is a short distance from the camp, at the mouth of Kalalau Stream.

An old sweat lodge constructed of bamboo and abandoned tarps once stood in the clearing next to the pool. Water poured over rocks heated by a fire created the steam for the Kalalau-style sauna. Ikaika mentioned an incident where there were about twenty people in the sweat lodge who heard a helicopter hovering directly overhead. Everyone came running out. "It was a good thing," he said, "because at that moment the chopper attempted to drop a load of seawater on the bonfire. It missed and landed directly on the sweat lodge, completely demolishing it." Such is life in Kalalau Valley.

A shortcut from the camp to Kalalau Beach passes the lava rock remains of a heiau (place of worship) located directly above the mouth of the stream. There are six heiau still visible in Kalalau. The two largest ones are located on either side of the stream; the most prominent named Kala. From the top of it there is a clear view of the entire coast and Kalalau Beach a half-mile away. Nearby is the site of the old Kalalau missionary school built in 1837.

The path meets the coast and converges with the main trail, which leads to State Parks campsites located in the milo tree forest at the far east end of the beach. Hawaiian men used the hardwood milo wood for woodcarving, and women pounded its soft bark to make tapa cloth.

Kalalau Valley and Kalalau Beach are part of the State of Hawai'i's Nā Pali Coast State Park. The Territory of Hawai'i made most of Nā Pali a forest reserve in 1907, except for sections of Kalalau, which were still inhabited by native Hawaiians. By 1920 all the Kalalau residents had moved out to enjoy the benefits of modern living found in Hā'ena, Hanalei, and the Westside of Kaua'i.

Much of the open land was leased to ranchers, but the leases were eventually cancelled due to the erosion caused by cattle. Makaweli Ranch, owned by the Robinson family of Ni'ihau and Makaweli, continued to barge cattle in and out of their 150 acres in Kalalau Valley into the 1970s. During that decade the state gained control of the entire valley and it was turned over to the State Parks Division. During this era waves of itinerant campers began making the valley their home. Before this, the valley was mostly uninhabited, with hunters temporarily entering, except for the legendary Hermit of Kalalau, Dr. Bernard Wheatley, who settled in a sea cave in 1957 and left in the late 1960s as the campers arrived.

The line of campsites continues on to a java plum forest. Flocks of native nēnē geese and wild goats often meander through the campsites, and seem to be quite at home here. The grounds are covered with an olive-sized purple fruit, which locals call "choke fruit," because that's the natural reaction to taking a bite of it. The old Hawaiians are said to have known how to make a delicious jam from it and also special royal purple dye used for tapa designs. In modern times it is used to spot the malihini who, after sitting around the java plum forest for a while, all have purple polka dotted 'ōkole.

Before reaching the center of the beach, where the state park ranger's cabin is located, the new Kalalau library can be found in a small grotto at the base of the cliffs. This collection of books carried in and left behind by campers sometimes goes "underground" and is moved to keep it from being discovered by the rangers, but this is where to check out a book, or perhaps leave one behind.

A flat, grassy area used as a helicopter pad by the rangers is located in front of the ranger's cabin.

The scene nearby resembles an old South Seas movie set. A comfortable hammock stretches out under a large kamani tree, offering a view down the entire length of the beach to the east, and the continuation of the Nā Pali cliffs to the west.

Further down the trail there are more campsites along the beach ending at the beautiful, double-tiered Hoʻoleʻa Falls. The cliffs here form a semi-private cove not far from the beach and it's a good place to wash off saltwater after an ocean swim. Avoid drinking from the falls, for wild goats live on a flat directly overhead and the water may not be as pristine as it appears.

A giant sea cave opens in summer up at the west end of the beach when the huge winter swells subside. In early morning or late afternoon, one can sit near the entrance and listen to the echo of noio sea birds chirping within. Native Hawaiians called it Ke ana himeni (the singing cave).

The last cave on the beach used to have a small hole in the back of it that led to a tiny secluded beach cove on the other side, but a major rockslide in 1987 blocked the entrance. Aerial photographs of the coast clearly show the cave, the slide, and the secluded cove just beyond it.

Some swimmers venture along the sea cliffs between Kalalau and Honopū Beach, which is referred to by tour guides as "King Kong's" valley after the location was used for filming in the mid-1970s. If you are not a strong swimmer, you should think twice about attempting this, especially in the winter. The current is extremely swift, and it is easy to end up drifting away from shore and toward the island of Niʻihau. There are no lifeguards at Kalalau, and pulling exhausted tourists from the water in the winter has become almost routine for some of the old-timers living in the valley.

Bobo used to run down the beach yelling at tourists, "Get—out—of—the—water! Get—out—of—the—water! You're going to drown and I don't want to have to save you."

The trail just above the west side of Kalalau Stream leads two miles mauka into the valley where there are so many interesting places it would take months to explore them all.

Significant Kalalau Valley attractions today are known by haole (Western) slang names bestowed by resident campers beginning in the 1970s. Ginger Pool, Town Hall, The Riverside Café, Big Pool, and Outlaw Pool are all names that have replaced ancient native Hawaiian place names.

Heading up-valley a favorite stop is Ginger Pool where you can take a cool dip. Although there are dozens of pools in Kalalau, this one is unique in that it is bordered by fragrant yellow ginger plants and laua'e 'ala o Kalalau ferns.

Not far from the pool is a fruit orchard known as Tom's Garden. A philanthropist, affectionately known as Kalalau Tom, planted it in the 1980s, and fruit picked from the garden has sustained many a traveler over the years.

Tom's Garden is also the substance of a modern-day myth. Novelist Goonan describes it in her Kalalau travel piece: "Squatters are periodically cleared out (of Kalalau) by the state, but one hears tales of an Eden of orange, lemon, mango and papaya trees somewhere, and of a ghost-like kindly man named Tom who lived there for years and mysteriously reappears to hikers."

Ikaika and I considered providing a map of the Kalalau interior for this book, showing the locations of the main trails and landmarks, but decided against it because it would invariably end up getting people lost. Besides, if such a map was published, the "secret places" within the valley would no longer be secret.

If you are intent on exploring the deep interior of the valley, consider taking along a guide. It's easy to become lost in Kalalau because the man-made trails and the goat paths frequently intersect. Another concern is the lack of daylight in late afternoon, for hikers neglect to take into account that the sun moves behind the huge peaks above Kalalau hours before sunset.

If you do become lost in Kalalau Valley, the simplest way back to the coast is to find a stream and follow it to the ocean. Along most of the waterways on Kaua'i, including Kalalau Stream, there are trails that follow the banks. At times these trails may cross back and forth across the stream, or may disappear altogether into a tangled mass of hau trees. The tendency is to solve the problem by forging ahead, or attempting a shortcut that not even a Kalalau goat would consider. If you cannot pick up the trail, then follow the stream bank where in summer, when streams are low, it is possible to jump from boulder to boulder. If you run out of daylight without finding your way, you can start a fire by rubbing hau sticks together. Although it may appear you are desperately lost, the beach is never too far away.

After living in the valley for a while, the walking, swimming, and foraging get you in good shape. One resident describes the Kalalau experience this way: "If you stay active here once you have arrived, you will develop what we call Kalalau legs. It's an even 10 percent uphill grade all the way to the back of the valley, so you really get a workout on these sorties. Before long your legs will actually feel strong, and the same trail that kicked your butt on the way in, will be much easier on the way out. It can still kick butt mind you, but it is nothing like it was coming in. You're in much better shape, your balance is better, your wind is better, your respiration is better, your brain is more clear—best of all you know that a cold beer awaits you at the end of the trail."

Seeing first-hand the sites where native Hawaiians once survived off the land is an intriguing addition to the Kalalau Valley experience.

Mid-valley there's a bluff area that used to be a village site where the elaborate taro-growing terraces are still visible. Near the top is a large 'auwai (irrigation ditch) for controlling the water supply in taro patches that would be opened periodically to water certain terraces. That was the Hawaiian way of managing water. It flowed steadily into the main streams, so that none was wasted and the waterways were kept clean and clear. From this clearing, about a mile inland, there is a panoramic view of the entire valley.

Near the main trail is a basalt boulder with a map of the valley cut into its face, showing all the major trails, kuleana (homestead), streams, and pools within Kalalau Valley. It appears to be very old, and most likely engraved in the same way as a nearby boulder with an ancient Hawaiian konani board (checkerboard) carved into its surface.

Throughout the valley are ancient terraces overgrown with vines. Archaeologists say Kalalau was likely the most densely cultivated taro-growing valley in all Hawai'i. If one were here with Captain Cook when he discovered the Hawaiian Islands in 1778 and looked into Kalalau from afar, all they would see would be green taro leaves glistening in the sunlight. There is no way of knowing precisely how many people inhabited this valley in the past, but judging from the vast archaeological remains it appears to have once been a thriving community.

Dramas of Kalalau

Cast of Characters

Anon-o-mouse—Poet / coward of Kalalau
Bobo—(Formerly) Known as the Calamity Jane of Kalalau
Bill Gladstone—Happy Rock / Po'haku Hau'oli / da literary agent
Goatlady—Catches and "decorates" wild goats
Guitar Rick—Brother-in-law of "nose flute" Claude
Hippie Chris and Wailani—Delivered their baby in Kalalau
Holly—Swims with the whales
Ikaika—Trail guide into Kalalau
Kalalau Dave—Kayaker and perennial resident
Kalalau Tom—Established the Organization of Kalalau Karetakers
Kalalau Steve—Established the first Kalalau library
Ko'olau—Legendary hero of Kalalau
Maki—Climbed 4,000 feet out of Kalalau
Mayor Ron—De facto mayor of Kalalau
Mead Head—Mead connoisseur
Noni Nancy—Noni connoisseur
Outback Jack—Opinionated Aussie
Da Grand Poobah—Kalalau chiropractor
Pi'ilani—Wife of Ko'olau the leper
Dr. Saldana—Former Kalalau MD and a story contributor
Sky and Radiance—Survived Nā Pali during Hurricane 'Iniki
Surfer Fish—Legal guru of Kalalau
The Kalalau Kid—Hiked the "back door" trail into Kalalau
The Plantation Mutation—Cockfighter
Dr. Wheatley—1950s–1960s "Hermit of Kalalau"
Yahoo—a.k.a. the Rainbow Rabbi

Natural and Unnatural Disasters on Nā Pali

The safety and security of modern existence seem to drop away as you venture into Nā Pali. It is just you and the elements in the most isolated region of the most isolated archipelago on earth. There are no cell phones or ambulances, and during the rainy winter season seldom even a passerby. On Nā Pali you are at the mercy of the elements whether it be a storm, or placid weather—nature has a way of reminding you of who is in charge. The following dramas are tales of survival on Nā Pali, accounts that describe the fierceness and wonder of human experience when faced with life-threatening encounters with nature.

On Nā Pali During Hurricane 'Iniki
By Sky

On the morning of September 11, 1992, ten years after Hurricane 'Iwa ravaged Kaua'i, another hurricane, twice as powerful, struck the island. A man known in Kalalau as Sky was hiking the Kalalau Trail when Hurricane 'Iniki hit, climbing the last ascent hikers face before reaching Kalalau Valley, an infamously difficult stretch known as Red Hill or Pu'ukula.

If I had to name one place in the world where I would not want to be during a major hurricane, it would be a toss up between a Haitian outhouse and Red Hill.

Sky recalled the day for me in a letter.

What makes planning a vacation so interesting is that regardless of how much you plan, how well you plan, and how together you think you've done your planning, the universe always has the last word! For three years Radiance had been reveling me with stories about Kalalau Valley—the incredible beauty, the incredible majesty, the incredible waterfalls and caves on a long, pristine beach. On September 10, 1992, after months of anticipation, our journey began.

I recall Radiance once telling a friend of ours, Aia Akula i Kalalau, "Don't space out" when you're hiking the Kalalau trail, pay attention. If you want to look at anything for a period of time, then stop, because you can really get hurt if you fall off. Of course, our friend did get caught up in the incredible beauty of Nā Pali, spaced out, and fell off the trail. He had to be airlifted to the hospital.

Mindful of this, we carefully negotiated the trail to the halfway point at Hanakoa Valley, where we made camp for the night. By the following morning, September 11, Hurricane 'Iniki, which forecasters had fully expected would bypass Hawai'i, had taken a sudden turn north to tour the Garden Isle. By mid-morning Kaua'i was on full alert.

Unknown to us at the time, emergency sirens were wailing and helicopters were evacuating campers at Kalalau and Hanakāpī'ai. In Hanakoa Valley, the trail passes over the jungle stream a quarter mile inland. We were cut off from all the rest of the world and had no way of knowing what we were walking into. Along the way I remember commenting on how extremely humid it was. Radiance, a fifth-generation Hawaiian, casually responded, "Probably a hurricane." I didn't take her too seriously until I began to notice that all traffic along the coast had ceased. The Zodiac boats and helicopters that normally could be seen or heard from the trail were nowhere to be seen. About one mile outside Kalalau we discovered why.

In a flash, the clear sky turned to darkness, and the winds picked up dramatically. As we slowly edged along the steep, narrow trail, the driving wind and rain felt like needles piercing us. ('Iniki literally means a sharp, piercing wind.) Now when a wind gust comes along and slams you and your fifty-pound pack into the mountainside you start having godly thoughts. When the trail you are on suddenly turns to mud, then disappears down the side of the cliff you start having godly talks. When the wind knocks your legs out from under you and you slide in red mud toward a 300-foot vertical drop into raging surf…well my godly thoughts and godly talks were carrying on like a minister at a Holy Roller revival!

This couldn't be happening, I thought. Both of us were having parallel nightmares. We were caught in the worst part of the trail, in a full-on hurricane and there was nothing we could do but forge ahead or be killed. I don't even remember how we made it past Red Hill, but somehow we blew into Kalalau Valley.

It was like walking onto the set of the Twilight Zone—abandoned tents, packs, and kayaks everywhere. Somehow we were guided into a cave and from there we could hear the high-pitched wail of 'Iniki gather intensity until it became a deafening roar. The great director in the sky apparently had waited for us to reach the safety of the cave before the dramatic final act.

One-hundred-and-seventy-five mile an hour winds uprooted trees and snapped them like twigs. Tents, kayaks, outhouses, and camping equipment came flying past the entrance of the cave as large boulders crashed down from the cliffs overhead. Awesome! Thank God we were safe! In fact we were in one of the safest places on Kaua'i. It was fascinating really. Birds, frogs, and other creatures took refuge in the cave with us and in that moment we all shared a common bond…survival.

After it was over and things had calmed down, I began to discover what Radiance was hoping to show me all along. As I looked past the twisted trees and wind ravaged beach toward the setting sun, I was so grateful to be alive and to have experienced this life-changing event. I could only agree with Radiance that, in spite of everything, Kalalau was definitely one of the most spectacular places on earth!

Five days later, after a wonderful time, with Kalalau all to ourselves, we were finally evacuated. From the air we had a first-hand look at the incredible destructive force of the hurricane. What used to be the trail was a tangled mass of fallen timber and landslides. Three quarters of the homes on Kaua'i were either heavily damaged or destroyed. The once blue-green countryside looked as if a nuclear bomb had been dropped on it.

Within thirty minutes we landed at the Princeville Airport, or what was left of it. The roof of the helicopter hangar had collapsed upon the entire fleet. The National Guard had set up headquarters there, and volunteers were busily assisting residents in need. One of them happened to be the same woman who we had passed on the trail the first day of our journey. She was delighted to see us and said, "I have been worried sick about you all week." All we could do was hug each other and laugh.

In Kalalau During Hurricane 'Iwa
By Bobo

The tales of Bobo on Nā Pali—a California girl of the '60s who settled on Kaua'i's North Shore decades ago—are legendary, and so incredible that it's difficult to tell which are embellished and which are straight facts. Most North Shore old-timers know and love her, and have a "Bobo" anecdote to share. One tale has her swimming the full stretch of Nā Pali—from Ke'e Beach at Hā'ena to Polihale at the northern end of Barking Sands beach—in her birthday suit, then hitchhiking back to Hanalei in the same outfit. She spoke of her younger years when she would swim from Kē'ē Beach to the beach fronting Kalalau Valley with her young daughters on her back.

Though now in middle age and a grandmother, Bobo continues to test her limits, successfully competing in the Nā Pali Challenge, swimming from Hā'ena to Kalalau, and running back the eleven miles of the Kalalau trail to Kē'ē Beach.

Bobo's "outlaw days" are over, but the stories of this incredible athlete and her tempestuous affair with Nā Pali remain legendary.

Whenever she is free from her busy work schedule, she returns to her first love—Kalalau Valley. One day she is an ordinary sales clerk at a posh North Shore surf shop; the next day she may be found in Kalalau Valley fishing at "Bobo's Rock," wearing nothing but the catch of the day.

Recollections of her experiences in Kalalau remain sharp, and like a star that burned out in ages past but still visible on a clear night, her light still shines.

This is Bobo's story of her encounter in Kalalau Valley with Hurricane 'Iwa, which struck Kaua'i in November 1982.

We had no warning. It was harvest time and I was living on the beach near the falls. My pakalolo was drying on the cliff, and I was just sittin' around smoking a joint when this mouse that I lived with started running around in circles. It's going around and around incredibly fast.

The poor thing was going so hard and so long, I couldn't believe what I was seeing. He didn't stop. He just kept going till he ran his little heart out—then he just flopped over dead.

I had no idea at the time what was going on, but I know now what the mouse was trying to warn me of. At the time I thought…man this is one strange acting mouse! But now I know the pattern. It was running in the exact shape of a hurricane! If you ever see a mouse doing that, you know a hurricane is coming!

The winds and the surf picked up radically, so I quickly gathered up all the pakalolo and put it in plastic trash bags. Then I headed for the big cave. There were about fifteen people held up there. By then you could feel the waves pounding on the shore like an earth tremor. I said to them: "Hey, I have seen this sorta thing before. We have to get outta this cave. I know the ocean will come up here." They all looked at me like I was crazy cause the shore was more than fifty yards away.

I took my little sister and said, "We're gone." We ran up to the second cave near the ranger station and built a fire outside. All of a sudden my baby goat runs to the back of the cave.

I'm like, "Hey goatee?"

And he's like, "Maa…maa…maa…"

I mean he is not stoked at all. That's when it hit. Rocks were flying past the cave like cannon balls and the palm trees were breaking like chopsticks. We only had time to gather our blankets and stuff when the second blast hit. It literally sounded like a freight train approaching, and by the time it reached us it was an all-consuming roar. This time it picked up the campfire and sent burning logs whirling through the cave like meteors. My sister covered her head and started shrieking. I grabbed her and said, "My sister doesn't scream," and she just...stopped. In those days she used to pay attention to me.

Meanwhile, those fifteen people I left in the big cave were in deep yogurt. By then a twenty-five-foot surge was pounding the cliffs. They had to wade out of the cave through white water that was chest deep, while carrying their packs on their heads. Some of them were nearly swept out to sea.

My sister and I moved to a third cave when it became obvious that it was too wet inside for my pakalolo. Man I was dragging that stuff all over the place. First, from my campsite, to the big cave, then to the other cave, and finally to the small, dry cave in the java plum forest where the tourists camp. Exhausted, but glad to be alive, I built a fire, curled up on top of my stash, and went to sleep.

The next day I woke up to the sound of a rescue chopper landing on what was left of the beach. They asked me if anyone was hurt. I said, "No...what happened?" I had no clue. They said, "Oh, that was 'Iwa." I didn't know what to make of it, and I go, "Oh, is it coming back?"

At the time I should have told the rescuers to evacuate all the people, but I didn't know that the trail was completely gone. Besides, I had two-weeks supplies, and I had no plans to go anywhere. Everybody else hiked out the next day, which is cool, because they broke the trail for us.

It was November 23, 1982, two days after 'Iwa, that my sister and I, the lone castaways, celebrated Thanksgiving in Kalalau. We found a ship's hatch that had washed ashore that we used for a dining room table. There we ate canned turkey by candlelight and watched the sunset.

Then we went up valley and it was so wild. It was the height of orange season and you know all those big, giant, sweet oranges that are at the very top of the trees that you can never get? They were all over the ground. Underneath every tree was a big orange carpet of oranges. We went up every day and filled our bellies. It was so cool!

Incident at Miloliʻi

Tuesday, December 13, 1977

It was the dead of winter when the Nā Pali Zodiac dropped off a party of five men at Miloliʻi Beach. Several days later when they had not shown up to pick up their gear, Zodiac owner Clancy Greff assumed they must have decided to stay longer and sent in extra food to them via Papillion Helicopters.

The following Friday the returning pilot reported that two of the men—Mark Allen, 22, and Tim Hacker, 25, of Hanalei—had left the group the day before to "find some goat's milk" and had not been seen since. Greff knew the hazards of Nā Pali and felt a personal responsibility for the campers since he had directed them there, so he attempted to organize a search party to look for them.

It was difficult finding any commercial pilot willing to go up in the stormy conditions, and only after Kauaʻi County Fire Chief Anthony Silva was contacted did a search party began to take shape. Silva quickly established a base of operations at Makaha Ridge, one of the few accessible landing zones in the area. From there rescuers landed at Miloliʻi Beach and spoke with camper Charles Defay.

Defay said that he had "a hunch" where the men were. This proved to be right on target and he was able to direct the rescue team to a nearby ridge where Hacker and Allen were found clinging to a narrow ledge about 1,200 feet above sea level.

According to the men, they had been chasing goats trying to "get some milk" when they ran out of trail. It began to pour and the stranded hikers could no longer see where they were going, or where they had come from. It was one single mass of mud for as far as they could see. Hacker said that at one point he slipped and would have fallen to his death if his friend hadn't caught him. Allen constructed a rope out of pieces of clothing and gradually pulled his friend onto a narrow ledge.

Because it had not stopped raining their entire time on the ledge, for two days they lived in fear that they would be washed down the mountainside. The landslides prevented any possibility of escape and not even the goat trails were visible anymore. All their efforts to signal passing choppers proved futile and they decided that if they were not rescued by Saturday, Allen would somehow go for help. By then both of them were experiencing symptoms of hypothermia and they knew if they waited much longer they would be unable to move at all.

After several unsuccessful attempts to get close enough to the ledge to drop a lifeline, pioneer Kaua'i tour helicopter owner and pilot Jack Harter advised bringing in a large Navy helicopter from the Navy's Pacific Missile Range Facility at Barking Sands, which was better equipped, Harter said, for a rescue operation.

This effort also failed as the pilot, fighting high winds and rain, repeatedly attempted to maneuver toward the ledge. He reported that at times the blades of the chopper had come within a few feet of the cliffs. There came a point where he was unwilling to take any further risks and said that they would have to find another method of reaching the stranded men the next day.

Harter returned to Miloli'i and explained the situation to the other campers. One of their friends pointed out that nearly fifty hours had passed, and that the men on the ledge had no provisions left. Reluctantly Harter agreed to return to the ledge in the rain to drop off food.

As Harter's chopper hovered over the steep face of the cliff with the supplies dangling from a 90-foot line, Allen grabbed hold of the harness and refused to let go. The pilot had no other choice but to carry him back to Miloli'i Beach. This method worked so well that Harter went back to the ledge and picked up Hacker in the same way. The rescue was completed by 3 p.m. and the two men were flown to the Navy base to receive medical attention. They were later transferred to the Mahelona state hospital in Kapa'a for a "psychological evaluation."

An Unsolved Mystery?

"Death in Kalalau Valley" a headline in the March 7, 2001, the *Honolulu Advertiser* stated.

"Police and fire officials flew into remote Kalalau Valley yesterday to investigate the death of an unidentified Caucasian man said to be in his late 30s to early 40s," the paper reported.

Local authorities were told the day before that a man had been found dead on Kalalau Beach.

In a March 10 follow-up report, the Advertiser headline stated: "Hiker May Have Committed Suicide."

"Our detective's investigation and the results of an autopsy conducted by Dr. Anthony Manoukian indicate he died of self-inflicted wounds to the neck" according to Kaua'i Police Department Inspector Mel Morris, the island's chief of detectives, who was quoted in the story. The report noted that the man was in Kalalau without a camping permit, and that his identity was still unknown.

Although the above newspaper account used the phrases, "appears to have died by his own hand," and "indicated that he died by self-inflicted wounds," the evidence was far from conclusive. Rumors still abound of what actually happened at Kalalau in March 2001, but news on the Kalalau coconut wireless indicates that it was anything but suicide.

There was talk of a conflict on the beach involving the victim the night before his body was found, and of a massive knife wound, which was impossible to have been self-inflicted. One perennial Kalalau camper stated, "Everyone knew who did it."

For those who were in the valley that night, it remains another unsolved crime on the Garden Island.

SOS in the Sand
By Loner

There were a few times I can recall when people wrote an emergency signal in the sand at Kalalau Beach. The first time it was somewhat comical. It was the middle of winter and this woman was so beat up by the trail that she wrote SOS in the sand to get a free ride out. She got what she wanted, but it ended up costing her several thousand dollars.

The second incident is hard to describe without getting too graphic. There was this woman, a supposedly brilliant lawyer, who broke up with her boyfriend while she was here and completely flipped out. I think she must have been on something. For days she would wander around naked and filthy from camp to camp speaking unintelligibly, doing obscene things and completely shocking tourists as they arrived at the bottom of Red Hill.

At any time you might expect to see her lying around in the stream or wandering up above, on the edge of the cliffs.

We were all convinced that she was a danger to herself, so we decided to call for help in the only way we knew how.

The next day we wrote a giant SOS in the sand and within a few hours a rescue chopper responded. When we explained the situation to them, they said that it was out of their jurisdiction and that they could not legally remove this woman if she was not injured.

Then, just as they were preparing to leave, they looked over and saw this woman riding on the tail of the chopper like a mechanical bull. That apparently was enough to convince them that she was insane, and they airlifted her out that day.

The third time an emergency signal was used it involved a terrible tragedy that I am reluctant to speak of because I was not there at the time. Most of the people in the valley knew the couple and knew that they wanted to have their baby born here. During her eighth month of pregnancy, they hiked into Kalalau. I'm not sure exactly what went wrong, but shortly after they made it in on Saturday, she went into labor and around midnight the baby arrived stillborn.

The next morning the people who lived on the beach wrote SOS in the sand. By the time the EMS chopper arrived at 9:00 a.m., the father, (known as Uncle T), had already buried the baby somewhere in Kalalau. It is a mystery to me why he was unwilling or unable to show them exactly where. According to newspaper reports, both the mother and the father were taken to Wilcox Hospital and then to the Kaua'i Criminal Investigation Division and charged with "concealing the corpse of an infant."

The couple did not have the $100 bail, so they remained in jail for some time. Meanwhile the State Division of Conservation Resource Enforcement searched for the body with tracking dogs. It was never found. The couple failed to appear in court for their trial, and even though the charges were treated as a "misdemeanor," to this day, they have never returned to Kaua'i to clear the record.

Rescue at Sea Cave
By Capt. Don Schwartz

I was doing a Zodiac tour of the Nā Pali that afternoon when I noticed a Boston Whaler with two couples aboard going by in the opposite direction. The winter swell was picking up, so we kept to the outside, away from the cliffs, and slowly made our way down the coast to Kalalau.

As we passed the sea cave near Hanakāpī'ai we heard voices in the distance. I couldn't tell whether the sound was coming from the cliffs or the cave, so I moved in closer. As I maneuvered around the entrance, which was covered with high surf, I recall thinking that no one could be stupid enough to actually be in there. The Nā Pali must be playing tricks on me. I couldn't see anything in the cave through the white water and mist, and so after ten minutes of searching we continued down the coast to Kalalau.

The Boston Whaler had actually gone in one end of the U-shaped sea cave and attempted to exit the other side when they were hit head-on by a giant wave. Their boat capsized and the terrified tourists swam to the back of the cave and climbed on the boulders. When our Zodiac passed by a few minutes later, they could barely see us through the five-foot waves breaking at the cave entrance. They screamed at the top of their lungs, but the sound was muted by the crashing waves.

On the return trip, I crossed paths with another Zodiac in the area. They reported seeing light coming from inside the same cave and radioed the Kaua'i Fire Department. Apparently the people trapped in there had recovered a flashlight and were sending a distress signal. By the time we reached them, the tide had risen, and the tourists were clinging to the top of the boulders for dear life.

Before long a rescue team arrived. We helped maneuver the divers to the mouth of the cave where they swam in underneath the sets and one-by-one rescued the stranded party. Getting them out was the most difficult part because the waves were so big that they nearly covered the mouth of the cave.

The most interesting thing was the attitude of the tourists. The girls kept saying over and over, "Thank God we're alive!" The guys just said, "Hey, what took you all so long?"

<u>Nā Pali Nightmare</u>

This was going to be the grand finale before this book was completed—one last trip into the valley. No one suspected that we would actually take part in one of the dramas contained within these pages.

International literary agent Bill Gladstone—who prior to the hike had traveled practically nonstop from California to Japan, to Hawai'i, to Budapest, and then back again to Hawai'i—was joined on Kaua'i by his lovely nineteen-year-old daughter, Tara, for the expedition into Kalalau.

Bill, Tara, and I had a late start that day, much too late for a leisurely Nā Pali hike. If we were to make it to Kalalau before nightfall we knew we had to keep a steady pace throughout. All of our supplies, including warm clothes and flashlights had already been sent ahead, so once we started, we had to press on to the end of the trail.

Unfortunately, I had a stomach virus, had not eaten for days and was in no condition for what was ahead. Tara, on the other hand, was a veteran hiker whose idea of fun was doing the "Machu Pichu," an extremely challenging high-altitude Inca trail in Peru. I knew by the pace that she set that I was in for a long day. Before we reached the halfway point severe cramping had set in. I kept assuring myself that it would be fine if I could only make it to Hanakoa Valley where I could find shelter from the pouring rain, rest, and get some much-needed electrolytes into my system. When we arrived at the Hanakoa shelter we found it packed with drenched hikers on their way to and from Kalalau. Without any significant recovery time, we crossed the swollen stream and pressed on toward Pōhakuao.

Tactically this was a huge mistake. Pōhakuao is the most dangerous stretch of the Kalalau Trail and there is no room for error. You must be steady and have a strong presence of mind to make it through safely. At the time, I had neither, and it took every ounce of my strength just to keep up with the Gladstones—whose name coincidentally is translated "Pohaku Hau'oli" (Happy Rock).

We were on the other side of a small, hanging valley, when my first fall occurred. I was hobbling along at a steady pace when I either stepped off the trail, or it collapsed beneath my feet. In an instant I slid thirty feet (head first and face-up) down the embankment. Finally I stopped my momentum by catching hold of a branch. About that time Tara had fallen too, and when she and her father heard me shout, "I'm okay," they assumed that it meant that I was okay, and they continued on. Meanwhile, I found myself upside-down on the side of a cliff, trying desperately to right myself, and spent what little strength I had left getting back up to the trail.

When I finally caught up with them, they had reached the most precarious part of the trail, near the seven-mile mark. It begins with a series of cutbacks over loose dirt leading down to what's known as the Crawler's Ledge, an extremely narrow path along the side of a sheer cliff. It looked as if we had made it past the worst part until we reached a place where the trail vanished into a v-shaped funnel. Tara stopped, looked over the precipice and said, "I can't do this..." I replied, "Can't spells can—although—not—trying. Come on now, take my hand."

This acronym didn't make much of an impression on Tara, and she steadfastly clung to the side of the cliff. At that point I took a deep breath, passed back over to her side, and gave her a lesson in Flaunting Death 101. "Tara just watch me. Put your left hand on the cliff. Then put your left foot here, and your right over...hereaaahhhhhhhh!"

In an instant I had slipped off the boulder and slid on loose gravel to within a few feet of a 500-foot free fall. Tara let out a primal scream, which startled me more than the fall itself. If this had been like the fall I had at Hanakoa where I slid out of control, surely I would have been dead. But, thank God, I suddenly stopped sliding. After pulling myself back up, together we crossed the gap and forged ahead, reaching Red Hill moments before dark.

At Ikaika and JaNee's camp near the mouth of the Kalalau Stream, we were welcomed with much aloha and a warm meal. The next two days were clear and we accomplished most of what we had set out to do. It was on the third night that we began to see the first signs of what proved to be the worst storm of 2004. Although the weather forecast had called for clear skies, I suspected something was wrong in the middle of the night when the temperature climbed from below 60 degrees to what felt like a sauna. It was strangely reminiscent of the gusts of steamy equatorial winds we experienced on Kaua'i in the hours prior to Hurricane 'Iniki on September 11, 1992.

By 5:00 a.m. 40-mph wind gusts began to pound the camp. You could hear the trees snapping up-valley and count the seconds before it hit the camp. Next came an ominous red dawn. Ikaika and I just looked at one another and said, "This is going to be a big one." By 7:30 a state helicopter buzzed the camp. At first we thought that it was another courtesy wake-up call, but the word on the beach was that they heard sirens.

Fortunately, I had made prior arrangements with a friend to pick me up by jet ski that day. There was room for one more, but Tara refused to leave her father behind to face the trail alone. He was the type of man who would rather face a Kalalau tempest than the Nā Pali seas in winter. I was a bit tense myself since I was carrying a video camera and the skipper mysteriously disappeared for an hour and a half prior to our departure searching for two swimmers that he thought had been lost in the current. Upon returning to the ever darkening Kalalau Beach, this tow-in surfer "hulied" (flipped) in the high surf. Yet he still managed to get me to Hā'ena safely that afternoon.

During the next few days back home on the North Shore I videotaped several weather-related news stories which aired on four Honolulu television stations: Kaua'i Braces For the Big Storm, Hanalei and Kalihiwai Bridges Closed, Giant Sinkholes at the Marriott.

I had reason to be concerned about the Gladstones when on New Year's Day 2005—the day they were scheduled to be out of Nā Pali—nearly a foot of rain had fallen. After the biggest storm of the year, it was doubtful that the trail would even be passable for days. Fortunately the next day was bright and sunny and the Gladstones arrived safely at the trailhead, a day late, bent, but unbroken. When asked about the trail, Tara happily reported that she was already well past the most dangerous part before she even realized it.

She told me: "It was something I needed to do for me. I think that is kind of what Kalalau is all about. You go in there with a certain state of mind and you come out completely different. It's really a challenge…an adventure!"

Perhaps if she had taken the jet ski out of Kalalau with me that day, the moral of this story may have been entirely different—something like, "There's always another way out." As it is, she discovered something within herself in the wilderness of Nā Pali, overcoming the worst of her fears in the middle of the storm, and being rewarded with a newfound sense of confidence having survived the experience.

Daniel My Brother

When island adventurers disappear on the Nā Pali their families often must face the disheartening task of finding them, against the odds and amidst a vast, rugged, and unforgiving coastline. Too often the search comes up empty, and the whereabouts of their loved one remain a mystery hidden within the dense jungles and the depths of the sea. There is always drama behind the drama for these families who are at the mercy of the elements and the goodwill of islanders whose responsibility is to find their missing brother or daughter or son. As a veteran stringer for Honolulu TV news stations, I've reported on a number of such family tragedies and usually try to insulate myself from them emotionally.

This particular search was different. My assignment from Honolulu station KGMB was to find and interview Susan and Ron Marks, who had flown in from Oregon to search for their missing brother, Daniel.

The twenty-four-year-old dropped from sight on November 10 and failed to show up for Susan's wedding held a week earlier.

Thursday November 24

As the interview drew to a close, Susan, a highly intelligent and articulate woman began sobbing inconsolably and soon had everyone, including myself, in tears. Then, as if angels appeared as tourists in matching outfits, an elderly couple interrupted our conversation to report that on their way to the airport thirty minutes earlier, they had seen a young, bearded man in a green sarong, fitting Daniel's description, at the entrance of the Tree Tunnel between Lihu'e and Koloa.

We rushed to Koloa, and from that moment on finding clues of Daniel's whereabouts became our raison d'etre. We posted fliers at all Kaua'i beach parks and tracked the unidentified man in the green sarong, all the way from Polihale at the end of the road on the Westside to Kē'ē Beach, at the opposite end of the highway. Every indication pointed to Daniel being in Kalalau Valley, if he was still on Kaua'i—which is what most locals assumed from the start.

The night before beginning our search into Kalalau, Susan and Ron received word that a man who had been following the story remembered having picked up Daniel hitchhiking and taken him not to Kē'ē on the North Shore, but rather to the Kalalau Lookout in the island's highland forest, a popular tourist stop located about 4,000 feet above Kalalau Beach. He recalled Daniel saying that he was determined to get to Kalalau Valley using an "unconventional route." This was also confirmed by a couple from Fort Collins, Colorado, who said that they had met Daniel at the top of the lookout a day after his last reported sighting.

When Susan and Ron heard that a positive identification had been made, their hopes soared. Susan exclaimed, "We needed confirmation that he was, in fact, up there, and now we have that!"

The implications of this sudden turn of events was difficult to explain to Susan without alarming her. "Suicide" was the first word that came to mind. Had they read the accounts in this book of attempts at scaling the "back door," they would have understood that sadly the odds were against finding their brother, dead or alive.

Susan hired Inter-Island Helicopters out of Burns Field at Hanapēpē to search the slopes below the lookout, while Ron hiked into Kalalau Valley via the Kalalau Trail.

Although their searches began on opposite sides of the island, the area concentrated on was separated by less than a couple miles. Bad weather hindered the aerial search and perhaps only served as a reality check for Susan who saw nothing in the jagged, uninhabitable terrain to give her reason for optimism. She sensed that Daniel was somewhere near and said after the flight, "He went in there from up there; he is between the top and bottom."

The next day, she chartered Jack Harter Helicopters. The pilot followed a ridge that ran below the Pihea Trail in Kōke'e State Park, and discovered an unmarked path that could have been used by someone determined to enter the valley from the lookout above.

Trackers were flown in from the Professional Tracking Services in Washington, and after a consultation with state officials who knew the terrain, they rappelled down the ridge to search the trail. According to Susan, they discovered multiple sandal prints along the way, which was encouraging to her because Daniel was known to have often hiked in sandals. She stated:

"They found prints in areas that were protected and unprotected by trees and they determined that the multiple prints were three to four weeks old, about the same time Daniel was up there. I would say they are ninety percent sure. He always liked a challenge, and maybe somebody told him it was not possible...and he thought it was."

On December 1 another search and rescue team made up of local volunteers and led by Charlie Cobb-Adams entered Kalalau Valley from its North Ridge.

The only encouraging news came from the trackers who reported hearing someone possibly calling in the distance.

Susan asked me to use the boom microphone on my camera to try to pick up the sound, but that plan was called off due to consistently poor weather conditions.

Every day that passed diminished Susan and Ron's hope of finding their brother, but they held fast until the end.

Lester Chang of the *Garden Island* newspaper reported:

On December 9: "Family members haven't given up hope of finding missing Oregonian Daniel Marks even though aerial and ground searches of mountainous terrain between the Kalalau Lookout and Kalalau Valley conducted earlier this week failed to locate him. But siblings Susan Marks and Ron Marks Jr. have decided a search will continue between the Kalalau Lookout and Kalalau Valley after professional Mainland trackers rappelled down from a ridge, found a remote and obscured trail, searched it and found 'multiple' sandal prints believed to have been made by the missing 24-year-old man."

More than seven months have past since the Back Door claimed Daniel's life. Susan contacted me from Oregon following his memorial service to thank me, and to send a CD of his music. In retrospect it was I who was indebted to her and Ron for drawing me out of the smug, detached world of news gathering and into their family.

Kalalau had become the crucible of all of their hopes and fears and in the end they found solace in knowing that Daniel left this world in the way that only he would have wanted to. They assured me that one day, they would return to Kalalau because there they felt closest to him.

Kalalau Outlaws

The so called Kalalau Outlaws, who occupy the Nā Pali Coast and Kalalau Valley do so without the permission of the Hawai'i State Department of Land and Natural Resources, the agency tasked with enforcing state park rules on this isolated coast. They are several generations removed from the handful of hermits, '60s and '70s hippies, and surfers who began venturing into Nā Pali some 50 years after the last Hawaiians occupied the valley. Some are native to Kaua'i, while the majority are from the West Coast and Europe. More sophisticated than the stereotypical Pacific Island "beach bums" of old, they inhabit this twenty-first century utopian community as if they were a law unto themselves. What the "un-permitted campers" living in Kalalau have in common is that they are operating outside state law and if caught they are liable to be ticketed, possibly arrested on the spot. For decades it has been a game of cat and mouse between the rangers of the DLNR and the Outlaws, who accept this moniker with pride. Just as the rangers have a job to do, so do the Outlaws, which is avoiding arrest while surviving in the unpredictable and often inhospitable Nā Pali wilderness.

The Organization of Kalalau Karetakers

Some folks call him Tom Bombadil after *The Lord of the Rings* character, because of his love of nature; some call him Kalalau Tom because of his love for the valley; and others call him Saint Thomas because of his philanthropic deeds. By any standard he has created a legacy on the Garden Island. Most people who hike into Kalalau Valley may not know who he is, but in time everyone learns of Tom's garden.

When he started his garden in Kalalau in the mid-1970s, all he had was the permission of state Department of Land and Natural Resources Superintendent George Niitani handwritten on the back of a business card. At the time he was only required to submit a list of the proposed species prior to planting trees. Over the next several years this garden was expanded into an orchard laden with breadfruit, papaya, avocado, mango, coconut, egg fruit, macadamia, malabar chestnut, liliko'i, banana, and an assortment of medicinal herbs and plants.

A decade later, on the front page of the *Kauai Times* newspaper, under the headline "Planting Another Kalalau Legend," there was an interview that made public what Tom's friends have known about him all along—he genuinely cares about people as well as trees. When asked why he does what he does, he answered unashamedly: "Jesus told me to. Basically, I'm just following directions."

Tom recalls that after 1975 the pressure to rid the valley of unwanted campers increased dramatically. "There were a couple dozen of us living in the valley at the time. I was the only one who wasn't growing pot, so I was living very openly. I cleared terraces and planted an orchard. So when the state officials walked in that morning, they found a beautiful place with flowers and fruit trees."

Since then Tom has been cited eleven times for illegally camping in Kalalau. He has always pled guilty and the fines and community service requirements have grown tougher each time. Yet, this did not deter him from planting, and even though he moved out of the valley long ago, he has continued to pack in seedlings either by the trail or by boat. A Nā Pali Zodiac tour company offered Tom a lifetime pass on its boats so that he could continue his work. "My gig is planting fruit trees and medicine," he says, "getting some food for the people in there."

In recent years Tom came up with the idea of The Organization of Kalalau Kartakers (OKK), a nonprofit charitable corporation whose mission is to protect and care for the flora and fauna of the Kalalau wilderness area. First he had to find a financial backer who would cover the $12.00 application fee.

With the paperwork complete, officers named, and fees paid, Tom Williams became president and founder of the first organization of its kind in the state of Hawai'i. He said it's "basically the expression of my love affair with Kalalau."

A quarter of a century after planting his first seeds in the valley, Tom summarized the work of the OKK:

"In May 1985 I founded the OKK with the main function of freely helping the state to protect and care for the flora and fauna of the Kalalau wilderness area and Nā Pali Coast of Kaua'i. Though the state has never contracted our offer of free help, the superintendent of the Division of State Parks at the time, George Niitani, gave me written permission to continue planting trees in Kalalau. We have been doing that ever since, expanding on the fruit orchard that I started when I lived there from 1975–1977, before the area became a state park. As time passed and enforcement of camping regulations stiffened, I began spending less time in Kalalau, concentrating on tree plantings on the North Shore of Kaua'i in public places along the highway and on the Nā Pali Trail. In May 1995 we expanded our activities to accept community service cases from the Kaua'i County Intake Service. While this regular flow of manpower has enabled us to greatly increase our planting and clean-up projects, the main function of our dealing with these 'criminals' has been in helping to rehabilitate them by educating them away from crimes and into community help—using love and forgiveness. To date we have handled 214 cases for a total of 14,700 hours."

Tom also expanded the mission of the OKK to include a food bank and a shelter for the homeless. Everyone seems to get along with him, the locals, the politicians, and even the park rangers. Yet he did manage to ruffle a few feathers back in 1993 when he circulated a petition to turn Kalalau into a "wild human preserve."

Tom stated in a 1994 the *Honolulu Advertiser* interview that many animal species have reserves where they are protected from harassment, yet no such habitat exists for man, whom he believes is the most endangered species on the planet. He said, "I'm just talking about a totally unrestricted spot where you can go and not get yelled at." Kalalau he referred to as a "free and limitless balm for the healing of mankind."

Talk of a real "habitat for humanity" caused alarm for some North Shore residents who wrote letters to the editor in opposition to it.

Addressing their apprehensions, Tom responded: "As a bonus the human preserve would be home to the 'riff- raff' of the island (toothless drunks, various outlaws, drug crazed hippies, etc.), and thus would eliminate the image problem for tourism. In fact a new tour could be added—viewing the riff-raff from the safety of Kōke'e lookout."

While it is doubtful that a "wild human preserve" is at the top of the list for the next legislative session, Tom's involvement in other Kalalau-related issues, such as helicopter traffic flying over the valley, has had a direct impact on public opinion. Wherever the battle rages, he continues to be outspoken in the defense of the Kalalau wilderness.

Besides being a source of food for the many travelers who have found their way into Kalalau, Tom's garden also holds a symbolic significance. It represents decades of success in proving his unwavering belief that a mere garden can make a difference in this world.

The Attack of the Killer Goat
By Da Grand Poobah

We had a situation three years ago when we were up-valley hiding out from the rangers who were looking for me. A herd of goats passed nearby, and at the time I was feeling a little boisterous, so I threw my machete at the lead goat, thinking I might get a free lunch. The blunt end struck it right below the shoulder and it turned around and gave me a long scowl. I didn't think much of it, and we continued on up and hid out for three days, as Kalalau outlaws sometimes have to do.

When we got up there we were sitting down taking a rest and my friend said: "Move!"

I said, "What?"

She screamed, "You better move!"

Just as I jumped, a big boulder came rolling down right where I was sitting.

She looked up and bellowed, "That goat is after you!"

I laughed and said, "Naugh...come on now."

We sat around for a little while longer and then the same thing happened. She said again, "You better move," and a huge boulder came rolling down the hill over the same area. At this time I was starting to get a little concerned. Within the next hour we had two more large boulders, and we're talking somewhere in the neighborhood of four to five feet around. If I had not moved I would have been dead.

What happened after that is sort of interesting. The lead goat came down about fifty feet from us and just stared at me for five or ten minutes. I kept saying to him, "I'm sorry...I'm sorry."

My friend was laughing at me thinking: "What's the big deal? This is silly."

Then the goat came closer and let out this big snort and the whole family came down and started eating right next to us. I promised myself that day that I wouldn't eat him or his family.

The Trial of Surfer Fish

I had to cut short an expedition to Kalalau to appear at the Hanalei Courthouse to contest a traffic violation. In the crowded courtroom I mentioned the name Surfer Chris to the man sitting next to me—a "patriot" type who hones his paralegal skills by challenging the constitutionality of petty offenses.

He said, "Oh, you mean Surfer Fish! He's on trial today after me."

Call it serendipity, or statistical Nā Pali probability, a man who had eluded me on several expeditions into Kalalau was going on trial for illegal camping on the coast. Surfer Fish, man or myth, was somewhere in the courthouse.

It happened that the same ranger who had previously interrogated Fish about his illegal possession of goat's meat was in court on this day to testify against him on an unrelated kayak caper. As I eavesdropped on the ranger's conversation in the lobby, it became apparent that he was in the middle of a tense exchange with none other than Surfer Fish.

It was then that I first heard Fish's aggravated, high-pitched voice echo across the lobby. "What…now I need a permit to go fishing?" The ranger, a tough-looking local, smiled nonchalantly and said, "Eh, that's not what you are here for and you know it, brah."

The drama shifted to the front of the courthouse where the county prosecutor reminded Chris of his many prior camping convictions. To avoid another trial, he considered pleading guilty to all charges, in return for receiving greater leniency from the court. I interrupted at that point, and suggested that he should plead no contest, and request community service in Kalalau. That way he could be in the valley legally and at the same time pay his debt to society. Fish eventually decided to plead no contest on one count, and to fight the others in court.

Before the trial began Fish spoke to me about his adventures in Kalalau. This small, inauspicious looking, middle-aged haole was relaxed and seemed to forget his problems as he reminisced about better days. With uninhibited pride he displayed the medal that had been given to him by a woman whom he rescued off Kalalau Beach.

As the indictments were read aloud in the courtroom, Fish demurred. He had been warned that this time the state would prosecute him to the full extent of the law. They not only had the sworn testimony of two veteran rangers, but photographs of his campsite in front of the big cave at Kalalau Beach.

As the ranger in his chino uniform pointed at Chris, identifying him as the one who had been caught illegally camping, Fish nervously clutched the medal hanging around his neck, kissed it, and snapped, "That's ridiculous—I saved a woman's life that day!"

On the stand Fish acknowledged that he did occasionally camp at Kalalau illegally because it was difficult to acquire permits. (Tour companies often buy them up in advance for their clients and the average resident can have a hard time acquiring one during the peak summer season.) However, on the day in question, he testified that he had kayaked in early that morning to surf and fish; in other words, just to be himself.

Although his testimony seemed credible, so did the ranger's. It was obvious to everyone present that the defendant fit the profile of a serial camper. But had his guilt been established beyond a reasonable doubt? Representing himself pro se, Fish had the option of cross-examining the ranger who had testified against him. He remembered the experience of being interrogated by him on camera in Kalalau, and used the opportunity to turn the tables.

Fish: Do you recall our conversation on the day you cited me?

Ranger: Yes, I remember you said, "Aw, you got me."

Fish: I told you that I had kayaked in that morning and I could prove it because my bait was still frozen. On the day in question did I, or did I not, produce ice-cold squid?

Ranger: I don't recall.

Fish: Did you touch my squid?

Ranger: I don't recall.

Fish: Was it smelly?

Ranger: What?

Fish: Did you or did you not smell my squid, sir?

Ranger: No.

Fish: Your Honor, I rest my case.

It was in the closing arguments that the state ostensibly overplayed its hand. The prosecutor stated, "In conclusion, your honor, the people contend that there is a logical explanation for the defendant having frozen squid in Kalalau Valley…"

Judge Rothchild, a man with a sense of humor, and some personal experience in Kalalau, interrupted the prosecutor and said, "Name one." In the end, she was unable to do so, and Fish's "Did you smell my squid?" defense prevailed.

Months later I ran into Surfer Fish at the beach and asked him about the trial, and his impression of the rangers. He replied: "The rangers…I love those guys! They keep the riffraff out of Kalalau."

"And what about that frozen squid?"

"Oh…one of the off-duty rangers gave it to me!"

Kalalau Outlaw

Following are excerpts from front-page articles published in Kaua'i's the *Garden Island* newspaper on the ongoing battle between Ikaika Pratt (who claims he has rights as a Native Hawaiian to live in Kalalau without permission) and the state of Hawai'i.

October 5, 2003—Hawaiian Cleans Historical Site Without State Approval

Lloyd Imuikaika Pratt's self-appointed mission is daunting: using a machete and a small ax to clear two heiau, one of which he calls the largest in the state, 11 miles from the nearest chainsaw, backhoe, or payloader. He has cleared nearly two acres of hau brush, java plum, oleander, and lantana already in the eight months since he started his mission. But the problems of lantana cuts and avoiding the poisonous sap of the oleander tree pale in comparison to his frequent run-ins with the state Department of Land and Natural Resources Division of Conservation and Resources Enforcement personnel, who have given him a number of tickets for illegal camping.

The state officers and Kaua'i Police Department arrested him September 11 on a bench warrant for failing to appear for an old camping violation citation, took him out of Kalalau in handcuffs, and flew him to jail. Ikaika for his part has filed complaints against the DLNR with the state attorney general for the neglect and destruction of the kanaka maoli sites.

Deborah Ward, DLNR spokeswoman, replied: "Currently there are no permits, licenses, or agreements to alter, modify, or disturb any historical sites in Kalalau Valley, or to camp without a valid camping permit."

As for Ikaika, he continues to clean the heiau as he awaits the court date. "Who gave me the rights? I gave me the rights. My ancestors lived here. This is our culture. This is our value. It may be overgrown, but it still has mana. It's really exciting to go and clean. It's like a treasure hunt," said Pratt.

To date he has found numerous Hawaiian artifacts including numerous markings on rocks throughout the valley (petroglyphs) and grave sites at two or three different locations.

Ikaika finds himself in an interesting mix: Since he has lived against the wishes of the state, he has become an outlaw—one of the illegal residents of Kalalau. He has become a friend and confidante of other illegal residents, and often settles disputes between them. He even banished one from the valley for drinking and the continual violence that his drinking caused.

JaNee Dominique, who has been helping Ikaika clean, said, "It's all coming together. He has given me the best example of living aloha, more than anyone I have ever met."

October 10, 2003—Ikaika Arraigned in Hanalei for Kalalau Camping Violations

In a packed courtroom full of kanaka maoli, native Hawaiian rights proponents, Kalalau Outlaws, and bewildered residents in court for their own cases, Ikaika pleaded not guilty to charges stemming from numerous counts of camping violations in Hanalei District Court. With people sitting on the floor, and peeking into the windows from the outside, Ikaika refused to speak to a lawyer, and a Hawaiian sovereignty activist draped in a Hawaiian flag was asked to sit down after standing with Ikaika in front of district Court Judge Frank Rothschild.

"I'm going to bring this to federal hands if I have to," said Ikaika, making a brief statement before the court. He added that he is a registered minister for the state and his nation and his "residence is Kalalau." In the first hour of the proceedings at least ten people were cited for Kalalau camping violations on September 11, the day Ikaika was arrested by the state for outstanding bench warrants.

November 13, 2003—Native Hawaiian Found Guilty of Nā Pali Camping Violations—Prosecutor Talon Spoke in Hawaiian During Cross Examination

After three different trials, the testimony of several witnesses, and numerous objections, speeches, commands from the judge—plus a lunch break—District Court Judge Frank Rothchild found Lloyd Ikaika Pratt guilty of two counts of contempt of court and two counts of state camping violations... The four charges can bring up to a year in jail and a $1,000 fine for each charge.

"This is a first step in a long battle," said Ikaika after the judge's decision. He had argued that as a kanaka maoli and a citizen of the Kingdom of Hawai'i, he is not subject to the laws of the state of Hawai'i and plans to file an appeal to the federal court in Honolulu.

"I am not in the state. I am in the Kingdom of Hawai'i sitting in my homeland. And you are foreigners," Ikaika said to the court.

Ikaika, who defended himself, was given leeway by the judge to present his case. He introduced a number of documents referring to the legitimacy of the court over a citizen of the Kingdom of Hawai'i.

Rothchild allowed them into evidence although he questioned the relevance of some documents, which included a protest of Queen Lili'uokalani, a civil suit against the state, and the presidential apology, signed by then US President Bill Clinton to the native citizens of Hawai'i.

"I am going to be liberal in allowing you to put forward these documents," said Rothchild, "since you are testing the authority of the court."

And for the camping violations, "This is pretty straighforward; I believe you have done good works. The system is flawed. This is the wrong place to argue that. I understand the nature of your defense, but the district court is not the place to change the laws," said the judge. He then found Ikaika guilty of camping violations.

Kalalau Characters

The characters of Kalalau live in their own world and are appropriately given otherworldly nick-names to suit their personalities. These may be indicative of where they are from, what they do, even what they like to eat. Following are first-hand accounts of their way of life in Nā Pali, their back-to-nature philosophy, and details of their sometimes comical misadventures in Kalalau Valley.

<u>Dances With Fish</u>

His name was Surfer Chris until one day Bobo's grandson, Dante, met up with him on the beach and said: "All you ever do is fish. You're not Surfer Chris—you're Surfer Fish!" The name stuck, and thereafter what people called him was an indication of how long they had been in Kalalau. For years he has been playing hide and seek with the park rangers and always has an interesting story to tell.

Surfer Fish's Filipino friend Hobie had killed two goats (with one arrow!) and had given him one of them. As he was skinning it, a chopper with rangers aboard landed nearby. Fish said he knew that he was "busted," so he ditched his supplies and continued working nonchalantly. Then the rangers allegedly rushed into the camp, pointed an automatic rifle at him and shouted, "Drop your weapon!"

Fish promptly dropped his skinning knife and tried to appear as passive as possible. He explained that a bow hunter who had passed by a few hours earlier had given him the goat. After the rangers discovered no other incriminating evidence, they confiscated his kayak and ordered him out of the valley.

About ten o'clock that evening Fish and Hobie were sitting around the campfire discussing the situation when they decided to reclaim the kayak. They approached the ranger cabin and saw the kayak lying alongside it. Just as they were about to grab it and run, they noticed one of the rangers sleeping on the ground nearby.

Hobie whispered, "Let's go for it." But Fish decided that a kayak was not worth the risk of getting shot in the dark, so they returned to camp. With renewed confidence the next morning Fish approached the ranger station and demanded the return of his kayak. The rangers refused and decided instead to interrogate him on camera. According to Fish, with the videotape rolling, they asked him for a detailed description of the "stranger" who had given him the goat the day before. Fish, of course, had no intention of doing this, so instead he looked into the camera and described the ranger standing in front of him.

"Uh...he was kind of a short, stocky, guy with black hair and a mustache...carrying a bow."

After the interrogation, the rangers confiscated some dried goat from Fish's backpack and cited him for illegally possessing game meat, illegally camping, and landing a kayak at Kalalau without a permit.

There is a somewhat happy ending to Fish's story. After being ordered out of Kalalau a second time, Fish camped at Hanakoa Valley where he met the woman who would later become his former wife.

Interview with The Natural

Holly, who is also known as The Natural, was an unusually independent young woman who succeeded in doing what many of her colleagues only dreamed. She entirely dropped out of the big city matrix to experience a life apart in the jungles of Kalalau. Holly brought to light some of the finest qualities of natural living, and despite the many challenges facing a lone woman in this environment, she actually made it sound easy.

What motivated you to leave everything to come to Kalalau?

I got fed up, quit my job, and just decided I wanted to be happy. However it was—I had to be happy. I was miserable, leaving work with headaches. I had been coming back to Kalalau and every time I was here I would not want to leave.

I would stand there at Red Hill and look back and just think…man, I want to live in this place one day and see what that feels like. To live free, ya know. So after these things shifted in my life I came for Thanksgiving and I said I'm going to stay back here for a month. I want to see what that's like. I had a little money saved and I don't have children. I want to check it out. I'm free.

And so at the end of that month I stayed another and another. I used to take it day by day, but now it's month by month. Another one goes by and I check in with myself and say well…what do you want to do? I grew up in the city, but I've always had visions of living in the wilderness. It is so dynamic here. The ocean, the river, the tropical rain forest, the waterfalls…you never get bored here.

How much of the valley have you explored?

Quite a bit. This place seems small but it would take years to know the valley…to really know it. I like to hike, so I hike. Ya know, I check things out. I get around pretty well in the jungle, but I don't feel I've seen everything yet, to be honest.

How long have you been here?

I've been in Kalalau since Thanksgiving...nearly six months now. At first I wandered a lot. That's what I love is the freedom of putting your sleeping bag in your backpack and sleeping wherever you wish and you don't have to pay. Ya know, the land is free.

This earth and the land should be free. So that's the beauty of just taking your sleeping bag and going wherever you go, whatever feels good, wherever you end up—you sleep right there. And so that's what I do, but I have a camp up-valley that I like a lot and I come here to the beach occasionally just to see what is going on.

Oh! Here comes the *Independence*. You know it's Sunday because the (cruise) ship always passes by. It's amazing you can be miles up in the valley and see it all the way down here. It helps you keep track of time.

What do your parents think about it?

My mom is coming out! My mom wants to see what the hell is going on. Yeah, ya know they're worried and wondering what you are doing at this stage of your life. You're 29, you have no possessions and you're living on a beach. They don't understand. They're in their late sixties. So I wrote my mom a long letter. She was real worried about me and I told her: "This is me. Accept me for who I am. Accept me...don't expect, but accept." She really took it to heart and my friend just hiked in and told me she's coming. I'm so excited. I hope she likes my friends.

How do you communicate with her?

I have to hike out every now and then, unfortunately. I'm not self-sufficient back here. That's why I say we need some elders and some local people, some people like Ikaika to stay back here. As far as I know, he is the only Hawaiian who hikes back here regularly. It would be nice to have others show us how to live off the land. I'm learning how to catch fish and for the first time in my life I think it's possible to become self-sufficient…completely self-sufficient.

Have you had any scary experiences?

No…never. The only scary experiences I've had have been with myself. This place is so gentle to me and so beautiful that it just totally takes care of you. I've been hiking down from the valley and had my flashlight go out and had to walk in the pitch black and take hours to get down. But that was just my own fears. There was nothing about the valley that was scaring me. Now if you want scary, talk to Bobo. She's a legend. I've never met her, but I want to. She's unbelievable. I wish she were living here now to inspire me. You should talk to Mayor Ron. He's a storyteller by nature. He loves to tell stories and it's the way he tells them that is so interesting.

One time he talked about how Bobo was out in the ocean, like way the hell out there, sailing with some guy when the boat broke. I'm not sure what. Basically they got stuck out in the ocean with no radio and they were drifting out of control. Then Bobo says, "Okay… wait for me," and she dives off the boat completely naked. She swims for like hours and lands on one of the beaches along the Nā Pali and falls asleep.

When she wakes up she finds a beautiful, large conch shell on the beach and she says, "I've got to keep this—I have nothing." She swims for another couple of hours and comes out at Polihale. There are no phones around and sure enough she comes upon this tourist and says, "I'll give you this shell if you give me a ride." He said, "Sure!" and she got a ride all the way to Kekaha where she made a phone call to the Coast Guard. Within a few hours they rescued her friend. She is one unique lady.

What was your day like?

This morning I woke up on the bluff and I saw spinner dolphins jumping offshore. It was so beautiful. It inspired me to go body surfing. The sunshine was hitting their fins just right. Whoa…I just saw something jump! There…a humpback whale! Do you see it?

Anyway, I walked down to the beach because I wanted to ask this brother if he wanted to kayak down the Nā Pali where you can get coconuts and shells. He said no, but we hung out a bit and were looking out and we just see these whales right off shore. It's a really flat day and I guess they feel safe coming in close. They're just right there, so I got inspired to go in the water with them. It was glassy and beautiful and you could put your head under the water and hear them singing. It was just magical…they are such peaceful creatures, and they love Kalalau. They pop their heads up and see what's going on here. I floated for the longest time just watching them pass by.

Later on in the afternoon Ikaika and I kayaked down the coast toward Polihale to collect coconuts and shells on some of the more remote beaches. It was incredibly beautiful, but on the way back we had to fight the winds and current.

The waves picked up and when we finally reached Kalalau we were up-ended on the beach. It was fun! Ikaika took the kayak out of the water there and we pushed it a hundred yards along a channel that paralleled the beach. Later on a boat arrived with supplies and we all helped to pull the containers out of the surf. There were at least a dozen five-gallon buckets full of staples and special ingredients for a birthday party that we had planned for that night. All in all it has been another beautiful day in paradise.

The Goat Decorator

The name certainly does not do justice to this extremely gifted artist, but in the interest of maintaining her anonymity, she was given this moniker because it best suits her unusual preoccupation with Kalalau goats.

I once met a man on Kaua'i who said that his "job was not judging people," another who said that he was a professional "hoaxer," and yet another who amuses himself by carving stone artifacts and tossing them in the jungle in order to confound future archaeologists. However, it was not until I met the lady who decorates wild goats that I thought that I had heard it all.

Talk a bit about your experience on the Nā Pali Trail.

Well, the first time I came out here I didn't know anything about the trail, or the valley and I hiked in with a seventy-five-pound pack during a major storm. I was guessing at the time that the winds were about sixty-five mph. It was pouring most of the time so it actually took us three days to get in. Each time we went around the cliffs, the bags would catch the wind like a kite or something and whip us completely in circles. That was so much more fun than on a sunny day! I wish it were like that all the time. It was exciting and made it more of a challenge.

What is your favorite thing about Kalalau?

The hike…I like the hike. I like how peaceful it is out here and how free. I wasn't as free with myself before

I came out here. It's hard to describe really. I feel much more comfortable lying around in the natural. I never did that before. That's my favorite part, plus the liliko'i (passion fruit), climbing trees, and the goats. I love the goats back here. I just looove goats. They come in so many colors. They are really fun to catch and decorate.

Decorate?

Yes, I braid their beards and put little collars around the neck. I have done this to five or six of them so far. Some of the guys, I think, are a little jealous because they can't catch them.

Why not?

Because you can't outrun a goat, you have to outsmart them. I coo them and they let me get near... near enough to grab them by their legs. They usually go limp and I carry them off on my shoulders.

Do you ever eat them?

I do. The first time I ever ate meat...actually I was a vegetarian for nine years when I came here to Kalalau. I caught a goat and killed it and it was the first meat I had eaten, and it was very good. I tanned it out on the bluff and made a big goat bag with it. It had all these shells on the fringes. It was a very exciting time for me. I have also hunted buffalo before. In Hanalei, Buffalo Bill Mowry gave me permission to take out an injured bull from his herd. I caught it, killed it, and tanned it right there in the field, and like the Indians, I ate the liver raw.

Anything else that you would like to add?

Yes, don't come out here to Kalalau. I want it all for myself!

The Plantation Mutation

They call him the Plantation Mutation. This toothless descendent of five generations of Hawaiian, Portuguese, Japanese, Filipino, Chinese, and Samoan workers was born and raised on a sugar plantation. His real name is Kimo, after his father, an itinerant cane worker who had met his mother at a Westside Kaua'i cockfight.

Folks called him "da Mutation" because he seemed to have inherited the worst features of every member of his plantation family…and then some. Yet he is well liked, and what he lacks in personal charm is more than compensated for by his uncanny ability to pick a winning bird.

Some accuse him of cheating at cockfighting by giving his birds steroids; others claim he puts poison on the blades, so that when it hits the other birds, they die instantly. He says his accusers are just jealous because his birds are better conditioned. To train them he would release his birds on the wild roosters on the street—an exercise he calls their "road work."

He usually shows up in the valley after one of his "derbies" has been "bus up" by the police. Kalalau, he says, is the only place where he can "relax, lay low, and get away from all the fuss and feathers." If you see him at all, it will be deep in the valley on the trails, late at night drinking mead (moonshine) and singing his favorite plantation song, *Okole Hau*, which loosely means a steel-bottomed pot used to make the drink, or "Fall on your butt from drinking."

Okole Hau

Oh get one beef wida boss man guy
Wen' bus da sucka right in da eye
No mo job I get right now
All fo drink da okole hau
Okole hau…Okole hau

Wen' mek me lolo
Wen' mek me pau
All fo drink da okole hau.

One night I crossed paths with him on the trail and he told one of the most incredible yarns I've ever heard:

You like hear about one killah chicken? Okay den... listen dis one brah. Dis chicken fight was in Kekaha, and da owner said dat everybody should clear da ring 'cuz dis one man-fightin roostah wuz coming out. An he's one old man, so course, no one don' lissen. Da one's dat stay in da ring, are still betting, so he said, okay.

What happen wuz wen' he put da bird down da bird it flew up, trew a couple blows, an hit 'em right in da heart. Da knife went in tree, four inches, whatevah. Da man jus' went pale white brah. So they pull'em out, call da ambulance. Kay? Dis true story now. On da way to da hospital he died—"make." An dat man-killing roostah ended up winning everyting!

The Boxholder
By Anon-o-mouse

Checking the mail is the number one mission in life for many of us in Kalalau. The problem is that you practically have to risk your life just to find out that you don't have any. First there is the eleven miles to Kē'ē Beach, then another six miles into Hanalei, where the closest post office is located. I suppose that a thirty-four-mile round-trip on foot through treacherous mountain passes to check your mail is worth the effort if there is something waiting for you besides bills. The problem is that in this age of e-mail, real letters are as rare as tofu at a Texas barbecue.

In the old days at Hanalei, unless you were a member of Hawaiian royalty it was extremely difficult to get a P.O. Box.

One had to settle for the dreaded general delivery mail. It wouldn't have been so bad if they held it for you, but all general delivery mail is "returned to sender" if it is not picked up on a regular basis. So at least twice a month I was forced to make this magical mystery tour into town, well aware of the fact that if I dared ask the postmistress to check my mail twice in the same afternoon, I might as well kiss my next package from home goodbye.

I thought my problem was solved when I met Boxholder—the only camper in Kalalau who then had a permanent post office box. He agreed to let a few of us receive mail through his address on the condition that they check his box regularly. This arrangement was going along fine until the box became so cluttered with our junk mail that when the bi-annual "box fee" notice arrived, it was mysteriously lost.

Since Boxholder had stopped checking his mail, no one informed him that the fee was past due, and he forfeited his namesake. He is now known ignominiously as "ex-boxholder" and is on the long list of boxholder wannabes. Meanwhile, the postmistress continues to look at me cross-eyed every time I ask her to check my mail, and my parents have me listed as a missing person.

Kalalau So and So

One of the benefits of staying here long enough is that your name becomes attached with Kalalau—as if you were the very personification of the valley. It evokes strange and exotic images, and rolls off the tongue with such fluidity that almost anyone's name would be enhanced by it.

Would Ko'olau the Leper be remembered as "the fierce brave one of Kalalau who single handedly routed the armies of the Provisional Government and lived as an ali'i on the famous heights of Kamali'i from whence the fires were hurled," if he remained a paniolo at the Waimea Ranch? Who would Kalalau Tom be, if instead of cultivating an orchard in the valley, he just hung out at Ching Young Village? Who would the Kalalau Kid be, if instead of scaling the treacherous 4,000-foot cliffs at Kalalau, he had taken the "back door" into the Kukui Grove Cinema? These may have been ordinary people until they arrived, but it was the sobriquet Kalalau that made them a legend.

The problem is there is no one to carry on this glorious tradition. Ko'olau died deep in Kalalau Valley over a hundred years ago. The Kalalau Kid mysteriously disappeared; the Hermit of Kalalau died at Wailua decades ago; and Kalalau Tom has been spending more time lobbying the County Council these days than tending to his garden.

Meanwhile, who's going to be the standard-bearer for the new millennium? I'm not suggesting that we should "Kalalau" every rube who wanders off the trail, but perhaps we've set our standards too high, placing too much of a premium on actions rather than words. If the name sounds odd then that's the only thing people are going to remember.

Bobo is the most likely candidate for a name enhancement. Like Kalalau Tom, she's a living legend and deserves the recognition. But Kalalau Bobo doesn't cut it, nor does Kalalau Yahoo, or Kalalau Surfer Fish. What were these people thinking? By accepting the first moniker that came along, they've blown any real chance for name enhancement.

There are only a few logical choices left. Kalalau Don the Librarian is a long shot. Kalalau Ron certainly has the right metier, but he already has an inflated title.

Most of the other old-timers haven't really done anything heroic since they left home. So that leaves only Ikaika and a guy named Steward—the man from Iowa with one testicle, whose only accomplishment was finding two sunrise shells in the same day. Ikaika is going on trial for the crime of camping, and may be "indisposed" for a while. So I guess that only leaves Steward. He has more than proven his worth, and would be the perfect candidate if not for his indecorous appearance and the fact that he would invariably be mistaken for Kalalau stew—which is something we eat.

It's important that we find someone whose name not only resonates well, but who can personify the Kalalau mystique—not the type who steals the Thanksgiving turkey, or shows up nude at Hanalei Court with a wild goat on a leash, or who lies under oath about frozen squid! We need someone from the planet sane, who has a clean record, no aliases, and nothing to hide.

If you think you know of a likely candidate, please contact our agent. Meanwhile, if you see someone fitting that description, just say, "Hey Kalalau so and so." Who knows, the name just might stick.

The Kalalau Way

How long, oh Kalalau, will the sun pierce my eyes
before I metamorphosis?
Shall I remain in this cocoon
a prisoner of fate,
or emerge from it with wings of dawn
free from this estate?
How long before the rising tide shall cover me with sand
with what remains of who I was entombed with who I am?
Arise…arise thou lazy slug! Pupate another day
and better hide that sleeping bag, a ranger's on the way.

They say that there are two types of people in Kalalau, those that put people in categories and those that don't. For those who fall into the first category, the following guidelines should be helpful in distinguishing the basic types that you may encounter along the trail.

Among the core group that venture beyond Hanakāpī'ai are: the adventurer who visits once in a lifetime, the rolling stone who comes and goes, and the lifers who don't literally spend their whole lives in Kalalau—just the best part of it. If you are going into the valley it is useful to sort these people out before you get there so you don't waste precious time on it later.

The adventurers are easily identified because they look the sanest, but behave the most like suicidal psychopaths. They plan their lives around placing it at risk. Yet if there is any equipment that will improve their chances of survival, they will pack it along—wild boar repellent, chlorine pills, and satellite location devises that can find you just about anywhere on earth except Kalalau.

They carry enough food and survival gear to keep a safari alive, but still stop along the trail to load up on guavas just in case. Every emergency is prepared for. In case of sudden drought, they are connected to a water bottle by a long tube that rests inches from their lips. In case of a flash flood they have inflatable tent stakes.

In case of hurricane they have gravity enhancers. These are the overachievers of survival and they come to Kalalau to conquer it like Everest.

The rolling stone(r) usually cannot afford such luxuries. Most often they are very young, and though they may not have much, to their credit they have learned to be content with what they do have. Their equipment usually consists of a flashlight, matches, poncho, mess kit, knife, the book *Be Here Now*, a sleeping bag, and whatever food can be crammed into a backpack.

At any given time there is a steady stream of them on the trail. By the time they reach Hanakoa they may have fallen a half dozen times and their packs may be so deeply embedded in their shoulders that the skin is growing over the top, yet like wildebeests they continue on their migration to Kalalau. To cross the stream in flood conditions may place them at great risk, but that will not deter them as long as the majority survives.

Rolling stones are not to be mistaken for adventurers. They usually wear sandals instead of hiking boots, they have no pack frames, and their water bottles don't look like they were developed at NASA. From every corner of the globe they gather in Kalalau. They are friendly, talkative, and regardless of how little they may know about Kalalau Valley, or Hawai'i, they feel inclined to share its inner secrets with you. If you didn't know better you would think they were lifers.

Don't ask lifers where they are from or they will look at you like you just insulted their mothers. They are from Kalalau and they rule like kings and queens in a land occupied by a foreign army. You won't see them passing you on the trail unless they want you to. But if they decide to expose themselves, they know just how to do it. At times these encounters are like passing through a time warp—modern man in a lost world searching for avocados.

Their clothing, if any, is strictly jungle wear; no camouflage, collars, denim, fringe, leather, belt loops, pockets, polyesters, plaids, or polka dots. A lava lava is fashionable, as long as it doesn't have something touristy like a humuhumunukunukuāpua'a pattern on it.

If you wish to engage them in a two-way conversation, avoid the subject of lasers, computers, or the Ultimate Fighting Championship. They are particularly disinterested in sports and entertainment unless it involves bodysurfing or nose flutes. They will tell you that they have their own entertainment, which is far more interesting than living vicariously through reality shows. They live in a fantasy world, which is strangely real, while rejecting the real world, which to them is strangely fantasy. If you want to know what's going on, ask them, "What's it like to live in Kalalau?" If their eyelids quiver before they speak, you will know you are talking to the right person.

If they offer you fruit, by all means accept it. To fail to do so would be a deep, personal insult akin to shaking the left hand of a Muslim. In return for the fruit you should be willing to pack supplies into Kalalau for them indefinitely. But, if they offer you a kayak for the day, by all means refuse it. That means the surf is over thirty feet high and there is no one else willing to risk it to fetch supplies.

You should follow them around for a while so you can learn how the system works, and find out where the secret places are. When I first arrived, I had to learn by trial and error. Eventually I found a guide, Kahu Tex, who for a price taught me "the Kalalau way."

The most important event of the day at Kalalau is the evening meal. It's always good etiquette to bring something with you. When Kalalau stew is on the menu, it's a "don't ask, don't tell" situation. Don't ask what's cooking, and don't tell them it tastes like rotten goat's meat if that's the only thing you had to contribute. If you say you are going to "pick up dinner," look for something fresh on the ground. If they pass around a cup of noni juice, don't spit it out into the fire. Just say, "Mmmmmmmmnooooni."

If someone else passes you homegrown tobacco, don't bogart it. Slowly draw on it, and then quietly comment upon how delicious it tastes with noni. Discuss the medicinal qualities of both. These are some of the more subtle ways to let on that you belong here. Kahu Tex says that if you belong in Kalalau it will let you know by not killing you.

Be sensitive to the people and respect their private space. If they repeatedly ask you not to dance around the fire while they are eating, don't pout. If someone is showering under the waterfall on the beach, don't sketch them, or make any personal observations. If you go body-surfing with them, don't say, "Heeere we go again," on every single wave and scream the whole way in.

Most of the Kalalau lifers have lived in the jungle for so long that they have the sensitivities of a wild animal, so any noise, even whispering, can cause them great angst. When gathered around the campfire, it is best to sit and think, or just sit. That's the Kalalau way.

On Nā Pali, there are jungle people and there are beach people. Usually after the beach people get their ʻōkole severely burnt for the first time, they become jungle people for a while. If you do hang out on the beach, be cool. When you are collecting shells, don't walk on the "shell line," and if someone is picking in front of you, don't cut them off.

If you find a nice sunrise shell, don't trade it for a giant guava. But if you do, be sure to examine both sides of it before making the transaction. Although these shells are worthless in Iowa, they are a valuable commodity in Kalalau—practically a status symbol. Wearing a multi-sunrise shell necklace says, "Look at me, I spent half my life on the beach and this is what I have to show for it."

There is also a social hierarchy in the valley, which is determined by how long you have been there. Newcomers are expected to help with the menial work of gathering firewood and washing dishes. But the more important issues are addressed by lifers who decide where dinner will be cooked, what's put in the stew, who is going into town for supplies, and which books should be banned from the Kalalau library. Jerry Falwell's *Mysteries of the New Age Rainbow Cult* and the *Spam Cookbook* topped the list. They later decided that a formal book burning was uncool, so over the next few months they slowly incinerated them using the pages for kindling.

A word of caution about camping in the valley...don't leave your personal belongings around the campsite, or the rangers will know that someone lives there. Spread them around with the legal campers, and then borrow them back as your needs arise.

Periodically the rangers stage surprise permit checks. If they do buzz your camp, don't throw guavas at the chopper and scream "Remember Ruby Ridge!" If you are caught, don't panic, and don't lead them to the hideout—even if they do offer you a free ride on the chopper.

Be like a chameleon. Above all, don't set up your tent on the ranger's porch and shout racial slurs at them while they write you a ticket. If you do have to go to court, see if you can arrange for a change of venue to a place where illegal camping isn't a felony.

Regardless of how many years of community service you're facing, don't say, "Well alooooohaaa!" before the judge pronounces sentence. Finally, if you have to do community service, don't ever volunteer for Kalalau sanitation duties. If you do, be sure to wear something...anything, to avoid alarming the tourists.

Once you have been here awhile all these things become second nature. Kalalau will feel like home and you won't ever want to leave. Even if an earthquake, hurricane, tsunami, or comet hit, you would want to be here. Kahu Tex calls it a "cleansing." I don't know what he means by that, but after all that community service, I could definitely use one.

Kalalau Collections

A fictitious account of one man's attempt to bring Kalalau fashions into the mainstream.

The idea of a Kalalau clothing line came to me in a dream. After months of planning, I finally found the courage to test my ideas in the open marketplace. With whatever we could fit on our backpacks we headed off for LA.

At the time I had envisioned us on a sandy, torch-lit catwalk with bamboo flutes and incense mingling with the open air. Instead our first gig was one of those spring break specials where rappers wearing sunglasses and wool hats, walked up and down the catwalk grabbing their crotches and screaming obscenities at the crowd while the models showed off their spring fashions.

All of our models were discovered here on Kalalau Beach, all naturals with real organic material in their dreadlocks. We started with the basic unisex outfit, a lava lava, puka necklace, and Niʻihau shell anklet. With their natural, rosy hue and well-toned bodies they stood out from the other models, who by comparison looked anemic.

Our models had their own unique style of slowly trudging down the catwalk as if they were searching for shells on a sandy beach. The tie-dyed Kalalau blue-dirt shirt and the purple polka-dot java plumb sun suit were among the favorites. But what caused the biggest sensation was what we called the Kalalau Sunrise Outfit. Its subtle colors of pink and yellow captured the beauty and mystique of the Hawaiian Islands. The entire outfit consisted of a single sunrise shell that boldly covered the navel.

Anywhere on earth that you wear this outfit people will recognize it as part of the Kalalau Collection. In New York and LA it is sold for $500 but while supply lasts, these rare shells can be purchased for half the price. To order an original Kalalau Sunrise Outfit please send a check or money order to:

Kalalau Collections
Attn: Estuary
General Delivery
Hanalei, HI 96714

The Monk Seal

There were only a few people in the valley at the time, and when a large monk seal landed on the beach, they all quietly observed it from a distance. Among them was a German girl named Naomi, who spoke very little English. She had been in Kalalau for a week, but couldn't leave because she was still recovering from her hike in. Her feet were so badly bruised by the trail that she appeared to have blue nail polish on her toes.

Naomi was sitting beside Mayor Ron, who on any given day can be found on this same stretch of beach. He is a man of large girth and if not for the fact that he occasionally moved, he could easily be mistaken for a boulder.

As the two discussed the seal, Ron informed Naomi that the monk seal was his 'aumakua. The woman cocked her head to the side and asked, "What does this word mean...'aumakua?"

Ron explained that in Hawaiian the word means a family or personal god. "Everyone," he said, "has a spiritual connection to an animal which is their 'aumakua...mine is the Hawaiian monk seal!"

Naomi paused for a moment. Then, as if a light went off in her head, she smiled and said, "Ah yes...yes...Yes! I'm sorry... but yes, you do look like the monk seal!"

Kalalau Stew

Everyone who has spent time in Kalalau Valley has a special experience, insight, or lasting impression about it. We asked full-time residents and visitors who hiked into Kalalau for comments and almost all were willing to contribute something to spice up the stew.

"The people we met were the best part of Kalalau."

—Tara Gladstone

"A man who swam all the way from Kēʻē to Kalalau told me he was given a ticket for arriving on the beach without a landing permit. All I can say is it's a good thing that he wasn't a monk seal. That could have cost someone a $10,000 fine for harassment."

—Loner

"I was in Kalalau in 1982 when ʻIwa hit. We had no warning that a hurricane was coming. Eventually six others and myself ended up in a little dry cave where we rode it out. Bobo showed up later. She came from the sea cave originally, but was driven out by the surge. They came up to the cave where I was staying. It was awesome."

—Kalalau Steve

"I don't have a hard time on the trail because I seldom carry anything that won't fit in this side pack. I don't even wear shoes."

—Kalalau Tom

"One day just before dawn several hunters arrived on Kalalau Beach by Zodiac and opened fire on the goats. The campers woke up in a panic at the sound of the shots wondering if a foreign army was invading them. Goats were falling everywhere, on the beach, off the cliffs, near the falls, people were screaming. I still have flashbacks about it."

—Sage

"One group of vegetarians who were camping upstream reported that they were awakened by a commotion outside their tent and were horrified to see a man tackling a goat and strangling it to death before their eyes. They were so disgusted that they packed up and left the valley immediately. I guess the guy must have been really hungry. My friend used the pelt for his drum."

—Micky

"My father and I are not that naturey."

—Tara Gladstone

"They call me Steve or Kalalau Steve, what-ever... not to be confused with Camo Steve—he suffered from severe jock itch. He always put corn starch in his camouflage pants to keep his legs from chaffing. You would see this white powder all over the trail and you knew that he had passed by."

—Kalalau Steve

"Kalalau is like a woman. One day she will comfort and embrace you and the next she will leave you feeling emotionally shipwrecked. I guess you just have to understand her cycles."

—Loner

"In Kalalau part of the daily entertainment is watching the kayakers land here. It is even more funny to watch them try to leave. Most of them have no experience with the ocean and sometimes need a little help."

—Kalalau Steve

"The valley has a way of humbling you. If you come here overly self-confident and without a healthy respect for nature, you may have to learn the hard way. If you watch and listen carefully to what is going on here you won't make obvious mistakes. If, for example, it's a beautiful day, and no one is out in the water, there is usually a good reason for it."

—Outback Jack

"Kalalau is the eye of the universe."

—Dalai Lama

"Not all the Menehunes departed at Wainiha. Some integrated into the system and I think the last one left when the Waimea Dairy Queen went out of business."

—Anon-o-mouse

"A tourist arriving in Kalalau with a large pack was asked what he was carrying that was so heavy. He replied, 'I didn't know what to wear so I brought a different outfit for every day of the week.'"

—Outback Jack

"Wailani and I loved Kalalau Valley and wanted nothing more than to have our first child born here. Her labor began during a major winter storm when the surf was extremely high. Aside from an emergency air evacuation, the only other way out of the valley was an eleven-mile hike along the Nā Pali trail. Actually we had no choice but to stick with plan A and give birth in the valley. When her contractions began, we boiled the water, battened down the tarps, and waited. The storm was not a serious threat and only accentuated the personal drama that only a mother can understand. As soon as the baby popped his head out, there was this tremendous flash of lightning, followed by Wailani's scream, a crash of thunder, and a baby's cry. It was like boom. Here I am! Both the mother and child were healthy and spent the next several months in the valley in what she has since described as being the happiest days of her life."

—Hippie Chris

"One of my most memorable experiences in Kalalau was attending the union of Ikaika and JaNee. I watched from the beginning how they set things up, the purification, and especially the very end of the ceremony when the double rainbow appeared. It was incredibly beautiful."

—Emily

"Another tourist comes stumbling down the trail. I thought he was going to fall over, his pack was so heavy. When he unloaded it he discovered that he had inadvertently packed two tents. Later a psychiatrist on the beach heard the story and surmised that the man had obviously made a mistake because he was far 'two tents.'"

—Bonnie

"My job is not judging people. That keeps me busy."

—Kalalau Tom

"I have no respect for people who are unwilling to stand up for what they believe in."

—Anon-o-mouse

"On the Nā Pali trail I would be so tired climbing up and down those cutbacks that I spent most of my time wishing them away. I would figure out how far I had gone, and how much further I had to go to the next rest stop and I just couldn't wait to get there. Three more ridges, two more ridges, one more ridge, and I could take off that heavy backpack and those soaked hiking boots that felt like lead weights. Then one day

I decided to enjoy it for what it was. I would focus on how good it felt to sweat all the way to the top of a ridge and then stand in the cool Nā Pali breeze taking in the view. I wasn't concerned with how far I had gone or how far I had to go, I would just enjoy it for what it was. At the head of the trail I would decide how many hours the journey should take and use only my legs to determine whether or not I was making good time. Not only did I enjoy the hike more, but also as my endurance improved; I was able to cut hours off my time. These days I rarely stop on my way into Kalalau because I noticed that when I do, I am more inclined to get stiff. At sunrise I leave and I am there by noon."

—Outback Jack

"I can't say I've ever felt bored here. What do I do? Just run around from one garden to the next, do a little work in each one."

—Kalalau Steve

"I use to hike into one of those mini-valleys every other week to bring supplies to his friend Maria, who was learning the 'Hawaiian way.' One day they were climbing out of a very steep box canyon when she slipped and fell. He scrambled down the cliff parallel to her, caught hold of her, and yelled: 'Maria...Maria... Pull yourself up, or two of us are going to die.'

'I can't,' she said.

'No, Maria, you can. If I live, and you die, your family is going to come after me. Now pull!'

'Okay,' she said, and she gradually pulled herself up.

I later explained, 'That's the Hawaiian way—no matter what, you survive.'"

—Ikaika

"Kalalau has become a spiritual smorgasbord with devotees from all the world religions coming and going constantly. You know you are getting close to the valley when you begin to see rocks wrapped up in ti leaves at various places along the trail, or tiny altars with fruit and flowers placed on them. If an anthropologist were to discover these altars anywhere else on earth but Nā Pali trail, they might conclude that a native made it. On the trail though, it is far more likely to be the work of a waitress from the West Coast who has lived here for a few weeks. Everyone seems to be on a mission here. Some inward, some outward, and some inside-out."

—Loner

"After being here so long you learn a lot about people. Out here they can't bring distractions with them. You learn what you can and can not handle. So many people arrive with the intention of living here, but very few actually do."

—Kalalau Steve

"To sit up there in the midst of that cathedral and to have to listen to these helicopters. Well, if that doesn't get your attention, you've got a real thick layer around your heart."

—Kalalau Tom

"People give away their tents, their backpacks, their clothes, their sleeping bags…everything. They leave it all because they remember how difficult it was to pack it in. You could start a camping supply store in Kalalau just with the stuff that people leave behind."

—Loner

"There is a sort of symbiotic relationship between the rangers and the outlaws, even though they are not aware of it. The rangers can't be there 24/7 like some of us, so when emergencies come up, who do you think has to deal with it? Who do you think pulls the tourists out of the water when they are drowning, or binds their wounds when they are injured on the trail? It's the people who live here. On the other hand, it is the rangers who represent the only law enforcement this side of Hanalei. Not everyone who wanders off the Nā Pali Trail is all peace and love and on more than one occasion the rangers have been there to remove people who posed a threat to campers. In general I think that if the rangers and the so called 'outlaws' could work more in cooperation with one another, everyone would benefit."

—Loner

"You know you are getting close to Kalalau when you start seeing goats on every ridge."

—Outback Jack

"The people living in the valley work to keep this place clean. I have seen it over and over. They are the ones who collect the tourist's trash, bag it, and haul it out. I don't think that anyone in government realizes that."

—Loner

"When people come to Kalalau, this is what they should bring:

1. Neosporin—The minute they get a cut they should douse it with Neosporin. The locals will tell you that noni will take care of the staph. It will kill it if you put it on right away and keep the flies from landing on it.

2. A good sunscreen—So your face won't end up looking look like a baseball mitt at fifty.

3. Food—Sure there is plenty here, but if you don't know where to find it then it won't do you much good.

4. Electrolytes—After hiking the Nā Pali trail you will need them. Most people think that the cramping that follows the hike is from sore muscles, but actually it is from dehydration and a lack of electrolytes.

5. A water purifier—A lot of people drink from the streams and don't have problems, but that should not deter newcomers from paying attention to the warnings. They may not have built-up a resistance to the bacteria found in these waters. It is not worth the risk of becoming ill and having to be airlifted out. Everyone is susceptible to leptospirosis, which can be extremely serious. Urine from rats, goats, and cattle have affected all the major streams on Kaua'i and if you have open wounds you should avoid the water altogether. In Kalalau the water is probably fresher and cleaner than most places on Kaua'i, but it is still a good idea to play it safe and either purify it or pack it in."

—Outback Jack

"A friend who lived in the valley once said to me that he knew he would never leave Kalalau. At the time I understood this to mean that he never intended to leave permanently. A couple of days later he went bodysurfing, and was never seen again."

—Ikaika

"These sunglasses must be ten year old. They're so scratchy, I hardly see out of them anymore. I need to manifest a new pair."

—Mead Head

"Sterling's last wish was that his ashes would be scattered at his campsite near the falls on Kalalau Beach.

One rainy day two of his friends from the Mainland found me camping at the river mouth and told me that Sterling wanted me to assist in his funeral. By the time we reached the site it was beginning to clear and a light mist was all that remained of the storm. We solemnly spread the ashes in the place the he loved so much at the base of the falls and said a few words. Meanwhile a rainbow appeared in the distance unlike anything I had ever seen. It was absolutely shimmering. For some reason the three of us instinctively stepped back and watched it as it slowly moved across the water, coming to rest just below the falls where the ashes were spread. We looked at one another in amazement. No one said anything; we knew that we were experiencing something indescribable. Slowly the rainbow moved back out to sea and disappeared. It was as if it had come to gather the ashes and take them to the place where rainbows go."

—Dr. Gary Saldana

"Kalalau beckons. At the lū'au, when the behemoth in the red tinsel skirt gritted her teeth at me, I knew it was time to go. They called her bro."

—Anon-o-mouse

Kalalau Celebrations

Celebrations have a tendency to draw out the Kalalau recluses who inhabit the interior, "secret places" of the valley and are seldom seen, or heard from, unless there is a special event. The backdrop of other-worldly pinnacles towering 3,000 feet above the majestic beaches and indigo blue Pacific adds a sense of drama to weddings, New Year's Eve parties, and ad hoc get togethers. News of celebrations in the valley spread like pollen in the spring. From the beach to the deepest recesses of Kalalau, word is passed from trail to trail, cave to cave, pool to pool.

Following are accounts of celebrations that seat you around the campfire at Kalalau, capturing the camaraderie and chatter that can only be heard on Nā Pali.

Have You Been In Kalalau Too Long?

News travels fast on the coconut wireless, especially when a special gathering is involved. I was looking forward to meeting some of the old-timers who were expected to show up for the birthday party that night. The plan was that after the supplies arrived by boat that morning, Uncle T, the cook, would prepare the cakes, and everyone would meet at sunset. This was an ideal situation for me since I wouldn't have to comb the jungle for stories anymore for all the old-timers in Kalalau would be together at the same place at the same time.

The supply boat arrived on schedule, but one of the five-gallon buckets that contained the sugar and flour was lost in the surf. Watching the recovery of the rest of the supplies was interesting and particularly impressive were the water skills of everyone involved.

At about 11:00 a.m. the cake making began and lasted till sunset. I wasn't too concerned that it tasted like stale noni burritos covered with honey; I was just glad to see that the long awaited celebration had finally begun.

The event did not start off too well as the conversation revolved around the qualities of homegrown tobacco, which was passed around the campfire like a joint. As a guest it wasn't my place to say something like: "Hey, I'm trying to write a book about how fascinating you people are. Could you please change the subject before I throw myself in the fire?" Instead I cordially listened and occasionally turned on my pocket tape recorder to capture gems like "the Indian medicine men used to use tobacco as an aphrodisiac."

Ikaika had already left with the only flashlight and I became concerned about how I would make it back to our camp a half-mile away across the Kalalau Stream. All I had in the way of a light was a laser pointer. I was standing ten feet away from the inner circle testing the laser to see if it cast enough light to cross a raging stream in the dark, when I noticed The Natural breaking kindling wood nearby.

Each time Holly snapped a twig, I hit the laser for a nano-second. Call it a juvenile prank, or a moment of inspiration, the circumstances reminded me of Mark Twains' novel *A Connecticut Yankee in King Arthur's Court* where a modern-day youth travels back in time to Camelot with a satchel of modern technology.

I secretly hit the record button on my pocket recorder and like an anthropologist experiencing a once-in-a-lifetime cultural phenomenon, I captured the Nā Pali "tribe" in a moment of absolute transparency.

(crack) "Whoa… what was that? What the…? Ron, come here! Every time I break a stick red sparks fly out of the wood. Look at that! Did you see that?"

Kalalau family—Kaluaikoolau, her son, Kaleimanu, her mother, Kukui
Kaleimanu, and her husband, Piilani.

A Kalalau military campsite.

Military burial in Kalalau.

The Kalalau valley community evacuated onto the beach.

Next to Kaluaikoolau's house in Kalalau— where Stolz was killed.

The Kalalau Library.

Campsite on Kalalau Beach.

Kalalau maidens, Tara and Sara, refresh at Ginger Pools.

Wild goat—a familiar sight in Kalalau.

Noni—the Hawaiian healing fruit.

Rainbow over "Red Hill," entrance into Kalalau.

Rainbow over the Kalalau "Backdoor."

Malihini.

Ke'e wave.

Acacia and Aaron at Outlaw Pools, Kalalau.

The "Kalalau Lookout" from Koke'e on Kaua'i Westside.

© timdelavega.com

Kalalau cliffs.

© timdelavega.com

Double rainbow over "Red Hill." © timdelavega.com

Kalalau sunset at "Big Pool" © timdelavega.com

"Yeah, I've never seen anything like it. Where did you get those sticks from?"

"From that big pile."

"Are you playing with me?"

"I swear to you brother."

"Get another stick. See if it happens again."

(crack) "Unbelievable!" Oh my God! Is it only you that can do that, Holly?"

"Nobody did it...it just happens."

"What are you breaking? I don't know what it is. Is it java plum or milo or what?"

"It looks like java plum bro."

"Shine the flashlight on the wood pile."

"This is not java plum, see the leaves?"

"It sure is."

"This is not java plum. That is java plum, but this definitely isn't."

"There it is again!"

"Wow! Look at that!"

"Everybody come. Everybody come. Come quickly!"

Some thirty people stand up and gather around the pile of branches.

"Hmmm. It's not happening."

"What's not happening?"

"There was a red light dancing over the milo wood, but it just stopped."

"Java plum."

"Forget about the java plum. I'm serious...watch. Something is happening."

"It's not going to do anything with you standing in the middle of the woodpile with the flashlight on. You're gonna scare it away."

"Break some more wood."

"It's gone. I swear we saw this...this...thing."

I swirled the red light in small circles over the woodpile and the crowd reacted in unison like fireworks spectators.

"Whooooooooooooo!"

"Unbelievable!"

"Whooooooooooooo!"

"Holy...Oh my God, look!"

"Whoooooooooooooooooooooooooooooooooo!"

"This is miraculous...It takes your head to another space!"

"There is something magic in the air."

"Naugh, someone has a laser."

"Be realistic. Who would have a laser out here?"

"Maybe the ETs have it."

"Don't laugh. I've seen the military do this stuff before. There's a strobe light on right now."

"But you never saw this?"

"No, I didn't see...I've never seen this. This is a brand new phenomenon. I've been waiting for this for years. There is something magic going on."

"Impossible."

"Hey! Guess what. Anything is possible... anything...anything. They are letting us see. The military can do what they do, but nature can do what she does and it's more powerful. It's letting us know."

"Show us more!

"Look! It's up in the trees! It's coming from the sky. I swear to God!"

"I saw it too. A red light in the sky."

"No, that's Venus."

"Man, this is phenomenal! I thought that Kalalau was pretty high, but I never knew it could get this high."

"It's a miracle!"

"Fer sher."

"Do you really think it's extraterrestrial?"

"Wait a minute, Ikaika told me this morning he saw the same thing late last night from his camp—a red light jumping around on top of the heiau. He watched it for thirty minutes!"

"For real?"

"Hey, you were there camping with Ikaika. Did you see it too?"

"Yep"

"Are you magic or something?"

"No...oh I've bent a few spoons in my day...but I was only scooping ice cream."

"Maybe we're all radioactive and we don't even know it."

"Maybe it's electromagnetic energy out of control. What do you think, Ron?"

"Someone just voiced an opinion that they believed it was a hand-held laser device. Do they have such devices that can do what we just witnessed? Cause I dunno, I've lived in Kalalau for so long. I don't know what to say."

"They've got those things and I think we've got 'em too. They use 'em in raids, but cleverly used in the hands of an expert...yes, I believe it's possible."

"It's an electrical thing I tell you. The military...I don't know what they've got but..."

"The Navy doesn't have that out here. They wouldn't do this even if they had the technology. No way brah. Sometimes there is a strobe light that you can see from the beach. But not this."

"It's spooky."

"I don't think it's spooky. It's a manifestation or affirmation."

"Of what?"

"Of positive things to come."

"We were talking about unity."

"Unity, yeah."

"Wow, there it is again!"

"I like the way they do it. This is real. There it is again—in the trees. Look! I don't feel it's a trick."

"I can't tell man. I'm wavering in and out."

"It's gone."

"I take it as a total affirmation, absolutely, uh huh. It's amazing! It's what everybody has been talking about and we're living it. Things are accelerated in Kalalau. We're gonna start walking into another realm!"

"Definitely in another realm."

"I have been speaking about it for a couple of years now, and I understand I am living my life archetypically. I can't...I'm not just Ron."

"Uh hmm."

"I might be part man—part goat."

"Mmmmmmmm goat?"

"Yeah...I might not die. I might blend into the forest. I might like sit on the rock and just keep playing my bamboo flute until I metamorphosis into the rock itself. I don't actually even believe in death any more. They say that it's a sure thing and that's why I don't want to believe in it cause I know how wrong I am with the weather. Death and taxes are supposed to be inevitable...right? Hee hee."

"Mmmm yeah. Your music will at least live on. We'll probably hear your flute like long after you're gone."

"Say Holly, lets go sit in the jungle and wait for it to come back."

"Yeah..."

The Millennial Celebration in Kalalau

The sands of Kalalau, like its people, come and go depending on the season. The beach is several hundred yards long in the summer with mild wave action. But its volume is greatly diminished by the huge north winter swells that smash into the sea cliffs, carrying away the sand.

There have been times when I have walked the entire length of Kalalau Beach without seeing another footprint, yet on this day—New Year's Eve 1999—there are people everywhere—by the streams, under the falls, on the beach, and in the ocean. A large catamaran drifts just beyond the break while tourists on board take snapshots of the thirty or so bodysurfers in the water. It dawned on me that since the clock had already turned over for the rest of the world, these people may be catching the last waves of the millennium.

I sat down and watched an 'iwa bird heading home after a productive day of dive bombing other sea birds. Their six-foot pterodactyl-shaped wings gliding on the updrafts of the folding cliffs reminded me of something out of Steven Spielberg's film *Lost World*. A magenta hue saturated the western sky and a double rainbow appeared over Red Hill. As if a curtain had fallen on the final act of a magnificent performance, a rolling shadow passed over Kalalau Valley, and I saw the golden rays of light reflecting off the peaks of her slightly rounded pillars as she bowed, then slipped into something more comfortable.

A bonfire was built on the beach and everyone was invited for Kalalau stew, which consists of whatever happens to be available at the time. This meal was exceptionally good because of the variety of fresh vegetables. In leaner days it may just be rice and beans with an onion added for flavor.

After dinner came the entertainment. The combination of bamboo flutes and crude percussion instruments was perfect for the occasion. No one showed any interest in getting drunk or shooting off fireworks. If they did they were in the wrong place.

The light show started just before midnight as the clouds parted, the Milky Way appearing to be so close you could touch it. Most of the people there had never seen the stars with such clarity and force, and we all shared what little we knew about them. I pointed out the rising of the star Hōkūleʻa in the northern sky (just below the Big Dipper) that signals the arrival of winter. The ancient Hawaiians called this the "clear star" as it stood directly over the Hawaiian Islands in the summer months, guiding the early Polynesian navigators from the South Pacific to the Hawaiian Islands. In the '70s a fiberglass-hulled replica of an ancient wooden Hawaiian voyaging canoe named *Hōkūleʻa* proved that it was possible to sail between Tahiti and Hawaiʻi without the use of modern navigational technology, guided only by the winds and the stars and the currents.

Rather than trying to seize the moment, we simply allowed it to happen. First the bamboo flutes drifted off, then the drums. We gave no thought of tomorrow, yet we were experiencing the dawn of a new era in the most beautiful place on earth, and we all felt grateful for being there. Aʻohe mea ʻima a ka maka (nothing more for the eyes to search for).

We sat in silence, listening. Then, as if on cue, a beautiful Lebanese woman with an angel's voice welcomed in the new millennium.

> And in the gleam of dying stars
> she captured the last of the light
> Then stole away the prophets say
> and kissed the earth goodnight.
> — Kona Lowell 1978

Thanksgiving in Kalalau
By Ikaika

It was about five years ago. We were sitting at my campsite and Bob was saying, "Maybe I'm going out. Yes...that's what I'll do. I'm going out to Hanalei and pick up some supplies for Thanksgiving."

Bob loved Kalalau because it reminded him of 'Nam. Usually he lived only for himself, but this day was going to be different. I think he found some satisfaction in the idea of everyone gathered together giving thanks to God for the food that Bob provided.

He left early that morning in an old kayak that he had found on the beach. We had no idea where it came from, but he managed to make it to Tunnels Beach at Hāʻena in it by midday. From there he hitched a ride to Ching Young Village, bought his turkey dinner, and hitched back. By the time he paddled to Kēʻē Beach on his return trip the winds had whipped up, so he worked his way to the outside, beyond the breakers. About an hour or so down the coast the waves doubled in size and he was caught in the impact zone.

The kayak jackknifed and sank directly outside Hanakoa Valley. Bob lost all of his groceries, his wallet, even his glasses—everything but the turkey itself. There was no beach at Hanakoa, and attempting to recover the turkey from the surf, he was pummeled on the rocks. Finally, he saved the turkey and dragged it along the sharp lava until he could pull himself ashore.

Bob was scratched up pretty badly and had to hike from shore all the way to the main Kalalau Trail, a half-mile up-valley. The problem was it was all overgrown jungle and between the boulders were deep crevices that he kept falling into. Sometimes there's no way of knowing how deep they are. These crevices are covered with weeds and may appear solid, until boom, you're gone. Many hikers are lost that way. They fall in and are never found.

With the twenty-pound turkey on his shoulders, he finally managed to reach the main trail, then hiked another five miles into Kalalau Valley. By the time he got to my camp he was so beat up I could hardly recognize him. His eyes were squinting because he couldn't see. His skin was sunburned, his legs were bloody, and he was twitching so badly I thought he was going to have a heat stroke.

Since my camp is the first one off the main trail, he left the turkey with me and told me he would be back the next morning for it. I said, okay, and he left.

Later on, Yahoo, who is "supposed" to be a rabbi, shows up. He's a funny guy—always saying, "Yahoo's the one! Yahoo's the one!" He would have what he called his "Yahoo sticks," spinning them around in a circle as he talked about himself. We called him the Rainbow Rabbi—loved the women—called them his "wives."

Anyway, after visiting for a while, Yahoo grabs the turkey hanging on the tree and starts to leave. I said: "Hey Yahoo, where are you going with that?"

"Oh…I'm cook 'em brah lala (over a fire)."

"What about Bob?"

"He said it was okay."

"Okay…bye bye."

The next morning Bob came back to my camp ready to start cooking."Where's my turkey?"

"Yahoo took 'em. He said he was going to cook it."

"What? You gave it to Yahoo? Do you have any idea what you've done?"

"No"

It ended up that Yahoo and his friends had a big Thanksgiving feast up-valley, with drums, bamboo flutes and dancing wahines. Bob was never invited, and ended up alone on the beach eating canned sardines for dinner. I heard that he was so angry about the whole episode that he never spoke to anyone in Kalalau again. He only left a note on his rock saying, "I'm moving back to 'Nam where people can be trusted."

A Unique Kalalau Celebration
By Bill Gladstone

On July 31, 2004 there was a unique celebration which further demonstrated the magic of Kalalau. Ikaika Pratt, one of the co-authors of this book had set that date for his marriage to his sweetheart JaNee.

Originally he was going to have a large wedding, but when word got out, literally hundreds of people decided they would attend. This would have totally overburdened Kalalau Valley since there are just not enough campsites to accommodate that number of people. So reluctantly Ikaika and JaNee cancelled their wedding plans and decided instead to have a special celebration dedicating themselves to taking care of one another, and to taking care of Kalalau Valley itself.

Only a relatively small number of people were invited to this special celebration, but in the end close to sixty people participated—which was close to the carrying capacity of the valley. Most hiked in, but some came by kayak. Many of the guests arrived a day or two early, and began helping with preparations for the celebration. No one knew exactly what to expect, but we all knew the celebration was intended to invoke the spiritual ancestors of the valley, and show these ancestors the seriousness of Ikaika's intent to protect the valley's heritage.

In addition to creating a special imu (oven) for the celebratory chicken and turkey dishes to be prepared for the guests, a large temporary structure had to be designed in case of rain. At the same time special sandals had to be made from ti leaves for Ikaika and JaNee to wear during the ceremony. It took four days just to make the sandals the traditional way.

Eventually the day arrived, and toward late afternoon Ikaika and his guests gathered by the mouth of Kalalau Stream. Both JaNee and Ikaika disrobed and anointed themselves with water brought from the ocean in a special gourd, and then in the cleansing water from the stream itself. Ikaika recited Hawaiian chants, and had all members who actually participated in the rituals given special kukui nut leis, which would allow those who wore them to touch Ikaika and JaNee during the ceremony. Apparently once the cleansing had occurred, and the first chants recited, both JaNee and Ikaika were endowed with the special powers of the ancestors, and even touching them could provoke an overload of energy.

Ikaika and JaNee led the way from the stream to the heiau, or temple area, above the Kalalau Stream. Once on the sacred site, Ikaika directly invoked the ancestors and gave them his prayer to protect their heritage. The ceremony continued with more chants and participation from specially selected elders to give the couple their gifts for long life and prosperity, so that they might maintain the valley and their relationship with it. At the end of this phase, the final part of this ceremony called for JaNee and Ikaika to move to the end of the heiau and to greet each guest individually, and to exchange the breath of life with each.

It was at this stage that an amazing event occurred. Just as the sixty guests lined up to greet the couple, a double rainbow appeared just above the valley, directly behind where the exchange of breath was to occur. The double rainbow endured for the entire length of the greetings, which was about twenty-five minutes long. Then, just as the last guest was greeted, the rainbow disappeared.

Of course, Ikaika and those who believe in the ancient Hawaiian traditions were certain that the ancestors had brought forth the rainbows as a sign of approval of the celebration.

Several guests revealed that they even felt the presence of the ancestors. I cannot be certain of that, but as a relatively objective, Harvard-trained anthropologist, I can say that the ceremony was authentic in many details and that the timing of the rainbow was nothing less than extraordinary.

With the ceremony complete, the guests returned to the stream site where dinner was served. There was even a wedding cake that had been created by some Kalalau residents using old style methods to bake without a true oven. There were guitar and ukulele players and much music and dancing. The festivities went on until the wee hours of the morning, and the valley itself seemed to glisten with a special clarity and purity from the stars that evening, and from the sun the following morning.

Back to Nature

Once even urban Honolulu provided enough tropical fruit and fish for naturalists to survive on. Today living off the land often requires a sojourn into wilderness areas far removed from the urban centers of twenty-first century Hawai'i. In a pristine environment such as Kalalau, native Hawaiian techniques and folklore provide an invaluable resource for not only surviving the elements, but flourishing in them. To illustrate this, Ikaika takes us freshwater and ocean fishing in the old Hawaiian way, and Kalalau resident Noni Nancy discovers a healing fruit growing abundantly in the valley.

Take Care of Kalalau And It Takes Care of You

Like most native Hawaiians, Ikaika was most at ease when he was talking about fishing. He says that he always packs his mask and spear when he goes to Kalalau because "it saves the trouble of hauling in a lot of food."

Ikaikai survives almost entirely by living off the land. To prepare for fishing in the Kalalau Stream he picks the bright, green leaves of the naupaka plant to use as an astringent to clean his facemask. Then he slowly slips into the deeper part of the stream and moments later usually emerges with a catch of fresh fish.

"Catching 'o'opu is easy," he says, "if you know how to do it."

An 'o'opu is a goby, a dark-brown, palm-size freshwater fish that spends part of its life in saltwater and is a favorite food of locals. Some rare varieties of 'o'opu swim in isolated streams on Nā Pali.

An 'o'opu is more likely found climbing up the face of a waterfall than swimming in it. By fusing its fins together, the 'o'opu forms suction cups on its belly, which enable it to follow the stream over smooth river rocks deep into the valley. It is fascinating to watch them underwater climbing on the boulders. Like salmon, all four species of 'o'opu begin their life cycle in the freshwater streams, migrate to the ocean, then return to their place of birth to reproduce.

Along with the 'o'opu, the prawn is another delicacy that is abundant in the Kalalau streams. They are found in shallow pools, basking in the warmth of the sunlight.

Most Hawaiians these days use wire traps to catch prawns, but Ikaika does it the old fashioned way by slowly moving his bare hands to scoop them up in the stream as he cuts off their escape route.

To catch ocean fish he uses a softwood hau wood floater with two eyehooks at either end. One side is attached to a fishing line and the other side to a line that is held from shore.

First he baits the hook with a black crab, then swims out about thirty or forty yards with the hau wood float. He sets the line at five feet below the surface, then swims back to shore and waits. When a fish takes the bait, it pulls the buoy underwater and gets hooked when it pops back up.

One day sitting on the rocks watching his buoy Ikaika was approached by a Japanese man from O'ahu who came walking down Kalalau Beach and asked what he was doing. "Fishing," Ikaika replied.

They talked story for a while, then all of a sudden the buoy went whoosh, disappearing under the water.

Ikaika jumped up and said, "Hold my flute, I'll be right back." He swam out, dove under, and found a thirty-five pound papio on the hook, then swam back and threw it onshore.

"Wow that was fast," said the man.

Ikaika then asked him, "Would you like to catch one?" He said yes, but when he was told that he had to swim back out with the buoy, he said, "Oh no, there are sharks out there."

Ikaika assured him he would be safe, and he finally agreed to swim out if they caught another fish.

No sooner had the bait been set then they had another strike. Whoosh, the log disappeared again.

The fellow was still afraid to swim out, so Ikaika accompanied him. When they got to the buoy, Ikaika handed him his facemask and told the man to check what kind of fish they'd caught.

He replied: "I don't want to. If I dive down and there is a shark, I am going to be really, really scared."

Ikaika laughed. "Don't worry, there is not going to be a shark. Sharks don't like crabs or people. They like fish. But if we stay out here around this fish we are bound to attract one shark."

So Ikaika quickly put on his goggles and dove down. Surfacing he said, "Wow, this fish is even bigger than the last one!"

That night they cooked the fish over a fire at Ikaikai's camp near the Kalalau Stream. The Honolulu man exclaimed that he had never eaten so well in his life.

Ikaika smiled confidently and replied, "Yeah, everything that is here came from the valley—wen' catch it, or wen' pick it up, or wen' harvest it. We get 'o'opu, prawn, 'ōpae, (shrimp) he'e (octopus), squid, shell fish, cherry tomatoes, watercress, katakmungai (lime), taro, banana, papaya, liliko'i, oranges, mountain apples, awa, coffee, all right here. You take care of Kalalau and it takes care of you."

Kalalau's healing fruit
By Noni Nancy

Oh noni with a hundred eyes how could I be so blind as not to see what lies within your ovoid shape and smelly skin? Warts and all—I love them too if only just to be with you to sit below your lofty boughs and contemplate your name...Oh Noni—Nonu—Nono—Bumbo, ancient healing way.

When my sister and I first came to Kalalau we camped along the beach in an area that had several noni trees around. My first impression was that this strange fruit looked like alien life forms in various stages of development, with their long, tentacle-like buds and odd shape. They littered the campsite, so I gathered the ones underfoot and tossed them aside. After a day or two I began to notice that they changed colors from a green, to a greenish yellow, to a whitish yellow, to a pale white with a flesh-like transparency. Some that were rotting even had a neon-like glow about them.

It wasn't until I accidentally rolled over on one in the middle of the night that I discovered noni's pungent odor. At the time I was a bit disoriented and thought that I had rolled over on something dead. Little did I know that this mysterious fruit would save my life!

The next morning I was astonished to hear my local friend Kawika tell me that this strange smelling fruit was actually a healing plant used by the Hawaiians as an immunity builder and detoxicant. How strange, I thought. We had come all the way to Kalalau for the purpose of detoxifying. At the time I was a physical and emotional wreck and my sister, Sage, was terribly obese. Perhaps we had found an answer to our problems right underneath us. Kawika suggested we pick noni when it's fresh, almost white, and allow it to ripen. Mature noni is called o'o in Hawaiian. When noni ripens put it in a glass jar for a few days and a very clear amber liquid will separate from the fruit.

Then take a tablespoon of the liquid every morning, and you may prefer to use lime as a chaser.

Although it took time to get used to the aroma, we soon began to relish every spoonful. Besides stream water, it was my only sustenance for quite a while. During those hot summer days when all I wanted to do was sleep, my sister explored the valley, surviving only on wild fruit. Even after our fast was completed we diluted the noni extract with lime juice and continued taking small quantities of it. Our days were occupied with body surfing, exploring the valley, and devising creative ways to just enjoy the peace of Kalalau.

That summer my sister lost over fifty pounds and went from blob to babe. In September she met the love of her life on the beach and eventually moved to Switzerland to marry. I was alone in Kalalau, and although I was a bit apprehensive, I knew I could never return to my former existence. For the first time in my life I was not dependent on television, nicotine, hydrogenated oil, caffeine, alcohol, sugar, pot, or prescription pills. In fact, the thought of them made me nauseous.

All of my senses were quickened and I was simply overjoyed just to be alive. I had stepped off the path that led to an early grave and on to the path of a healthy, happy life. It was wonderful!

Noni had, in effect, become my "drug" of choice. I spent my days gathering the fruit, preparing it, and researching its medicinal qualities. Although I am not a scientist or researcher, I gathered a great deal of information and recorded it in a journal, which I plan to publish one day.

Most interesting to me was the fact that noni is used around the world. Other names it is known by are nomu, nono, noni apple, Indian mulberry, bumboo, lada, and morinda citrifolia. No one knows exactly what the name means, but wherever it grew the surrounding cultures adopted it for medicine.

Kalalau Tom, who grows herbs and medicines in the valley, claimed to have once healed a woman of breast cancer by applying the noni poultice on her tumor. Another man I met in the valley, who is an expert in the use of Hawaiian herbs in healing, said that he cured a woman of stomach cancer using noni extract. I believe that this or some other heretofore unknown Hawaiian plant may one day provide the medical miracle that the world has been waiting for.

Most trees flower before they yield fruit. The fruit matures only after the flowers have withered away and fallen off. With noni the fruit (or receptacle) appears first, between two leaves. Soon afterwards, tiny, white flowers begin to surface on its face. They look like cute little tentacles before they bloom.

This fruit contains both male (pollen bearing) and female (ovary bearing) parts—which I guess insures that it will never be lonely. Each flower leaves an "eye" in its place, and each eye is actually a separate fruit bordered by geometric outlines. If the flower had five petals it forms a pentagon. If the flower had six petals it forms a hexagon. There is no logical reason for this inconsistency other than the fact that noni does exactly as it pleases.

It fruits before it flowers, reproduces itself shamelessly, and then arbitrarily decides which geometric design will border its eye. It looks like an alien, acts like an alien, and smells like an alien. And if it's not an alien, then it ought to be declared one.

A word of caution: Noni is a powerful substance, which is to be taken with a healthy dose of common sense. As it breaks down it produces an abundance of bacteria, and if taken in too large a dose, could be harmful to your health.

If you want to experiment with how your body reacts to it you may prefer to start with noni tea made from the yellow leaves of the tree.

If you take the amber liquid do it in small quantities and continue with it only if you feel good. Your body is the most amazing healing machine in the world, and if you listen to it carefully, most of the time it will tell you exactly what you need to know.

Twilight Encounter

'Twas twilight in Kalalau when I was awakened
by a tiny pinch on my butt
that I pretended not to feel
On those hot summer nights
nothing separated me from the Milky Way
Bathed in starlight
I listened to the ancient drone of the sea
as it slowly slapped itself
into unconsciousness . . .
The sensuality of the stars
and the pallid light of the full moon
soothed me like a balm
A nibble on my neck sent shivers down my spine
and though alarmed I remained perfectly still
save the pounding in my breast
Sensing small steps approaching in the distance
I closed my eyes and waited
So dumb...yet so vulnerable
Another pinch and I screamed bloody murder
coming face to face with a mob of ravenous
sand crabs lured inexorably by the smell
of noni on my lips

—Noni Nancy 2003

Kalalau Back Door

Most Kaua'i locals have heard of the ancient pathway between Kōke'e and Kalalau Valley (known in English as the back door, and in Hawaiian as kalou or the hook). It was never recorded on a map, but it appears to be connected to the old Wainiha Trail to Kōke'e, which also forms a long hook.

The last known persons to have hiked the back door took eight days to do what the Hawaiians used to do in one or two. The old trails may no longer exit, but that hasn't prevented modern-day explorers from trying to find them despite the dangers involved. Historian Frederick Wichman of Hā'ena states that "several skeletons of hikers who tried to descend to the valley floor have been discovered at the bottom." A member of the last Hawaiian family who lived in Kalalau says that these days "not even a ghost would attempt that trail."

The Hawaiians called a similar Kalalau path, Kealaka'ilio, "dogs trail," leading down to a steep ridge named Kapea, which translates as scrotum. Two other lesser-known paths follow along the eastern branch of the valley. One is appropriately named Kanau which means chewed. The other leads up to a very steep ridge called Kaloa which means dashed along the way.

In the early 1970s there was a man from Hanapepe known as the Kalalau Kid who was said to have gone back and forth between Kalalau and the Westside via the northeast face of the valley. According to Kalalau Tom, there was another loner named Chacho Rivera who knew of several different ways into Kalalau. His favorite was to follow the ridge formed by Waimakemake Falls below the Kalalau Lookout at Kōke'e.

Other climbers who have accomplished this incredible feat include Herman Mederios and Charles Nakamura from the Hawaiian Trail and Mountain Club.

An elderly man named Silver K. Pi'iwale and his companion William K. Hussey of Hā'ena also succeeded in climbing the Kalalau pali to Kōke'e. What they anticipated as a three-day journey actually took five. When they failed to return on time, a search and rescue team was dispatched, which eventually found them at the Kōke'e Park headquarters.

They walked in late in the afternoon and reported, "We are the missing persons." Pi'iwale said that inclement weather and passages that were completely eroded away held them up. Often they had to shed their backpacks in order to climb unhindered, and then they would haul them up by ropes. At times, they said, it took them hours to navigate short distances along the jagged passes. In 1972 Silver Pi'iwale celebrated his seventy-second birthday by hiking to the Ko'olau Summit, and repeated most of the feat when he turned seventy-eight.

On the way into Kalalau on my first expedition, I spoke with Bobo about the back door, and asked if she knew of anyone who had attempted to hike it. She said: "Oh yeah, sure, I've done it, but I'll never, never do that again! Never! I was so scared, I thought for sure I was going to die!"

The *Garden Island* newspaper reported the story of two brothers who attempted this feat and failed in "The Path of No Return," an article published in the summer of 1975.

At the time that they signed out at the Kōke'e Ranger Station, no one was around to warn David Reisner and his brother, Ronald, that what they were planning to do was nothing short of suicide. Early that morning the teenage boys began a 4,000 ft. descent from Kōke'e into Kalalau Valley with nothing but a rope and two day's supply of food.

They had heard about the legendary back door and had been told by a "frienemy" that it was "a cool thing to do." Instead of using the path that follows the western ridge of

Kalalau, the boys went straight down from Kōke'e. At 2,000 feet they became stranded on a narrow ledge.

It was impossible for them to go up, down, or sideways, and they were unable to even see what was below them. That night they remained huddled together on the ledge in a torrent of rain hoping that the next day someone would report them missing or a passing tour helicopter would spot them. Neither happened. Even if the rangers had been aware of their stunt, they had no way of knowing whether they made it into the valley and hiked out along the Kalalau trail, or not. No one would have suspected that they would be foolish enough to go straight down with nothing more than a rope.

Wednesday, August 27

After seven days of torrential rain, rock slides, wind and cold, they had finally reached their limit and knew that they had to try something soon, or else die from exposure. Their only hope had been that someone would spot their signal fire or the clothes that they had strewn over the cliffs. Nothing happened and they finally resolved that the next morning David, the more experienced climber of the two, would go for help.

Thursday, August 28

David tied off to a heavy log, and then attached the rope to his older brother's wrist. His plan was to rappel over the ledge on to what they had hoped would be another ledge below them. During the process of setting up the descent, a passing helicopter pilot spotted their bright, red blanket. He promptly reported what appeared to be a "hang glider in distress." A Kenai Helicopter was called in and rescue pilot James Purnell was dispatched to Kalalau.

Unaware that help was on the way, David lowered himself over the ledge. Instantly the rope snapped, and that was the last time Ronald saw his brother alive. The long silence was interrupted only by the arrival of the rescue chopper overhead.

In extremely dangerous flying conditions the pilot maneuvered close enough to the cliff face to drop a net to Ronald. He said, "It was awfully tight with the chopper blades in so close to the cliff. Then, after being carried out of the valley and over Kalalau beach, the unthinkable happened. The net holding Ronald broke free, dropping the youth 40 feet below."

Rumors circulated that it was actually a news cameraman on board who inadvertently hit the release lever of the harness while filming, but this is unsubstantiated. As a result of the fall, Ronald sustained several broken bones, and was airlifted to Wilcox Hospital. He still had the rope attached to his wrist as he pleaded with his rescuers to continue their search for his brother.

Friday, August 29

Fire Chief Rita assembled a rescue team consisting of the most skilled climbers available. They were flown to the base of the valley and attempted unsuccessfully to scale the vertical cliffs. Meanwhile, a Coast Guard helicopter, hampered by fog and drizzle, also aided in the search. At the end of the day there was still no sign of the missing teenager.

Saturday, August 30

Chief Rita sent out a call for additional help, and a professional rescue team from the Honolulu Fire Department responded to the call. They attempted to reach the ledge by climbing down the cliffs, but were unable to because most of the trees were too unstable to offer them any support. The effort had to be called off due to darkness.

Sunday, August 31

The following day they flew in and around the valley taking pictures of the entire area that they planned to cover. After assessing the situation and determining a route for each of the eleven rescuers, they elected to have the Kaua'i team work their way up from the base of the valley, and the Honolulu team worked their way down from Kōke'e. If they were successful in reaching the boy, he would be lowered to the men positioned along the cliffs below.

With nylon ropes the Honolulu team rappelled the face of the 4,000-foot cliff. The descent was extremely slippery and dangerous as they zigzagged back and forth between the jagged rocks. Late that afternoon they found the body of eighteen-year-old David Reisner in a crevice at the bottom of a waterfall approximately 350 feet below the place where he and his brother had spent the previous eight days.

Darkness was approaching and there was not enough time to evacuate the body, so the rescuers remained there on the ledge overnight with David. The Kaua'i team also camped below them on the cliffs in order to be ready to provide support from below at first light.

Monday, September 1

Slowly the crew worked their way down the cliffs, with the men below supporting the body as the firemen lowered it down by ropes. By 1 p.m. the 11 men reached the valley floor. Chief Rita said later at a press conference: "It is difficult to make so many decisions when you are responsible for so many people over a five day period of time. But I have nothing but praise for all the men involved, and we learned a lot from the Honolulu team on the most dangerous and expensive rescue mission we have ever undertaken."

Exiting the Back Door
By David Maki

David Maki and I met on the set of the movie To End
All Wars, *filmed on Kaua'i in 1999. We played British POWs
held in a Japanese concentration camp in Thailand during
World War II, a replica of which was built by filmmakers deep in a
valley behind Koloa town.*

*Maki was fifty-five years old at the time of filming, and weighed
what looked like about fifty-five pounds. His gaunt frame, garbed only
in a white loincloth, became the key image in posters for the film. He
was ignominiously known as Mango on the set because mango were
all he ever ate. This is his amazing story of a hike from Kalalau Valley
up to the Kōke'e Lookout.*

I was born on O'ahu in 1944. My mother was Japanese and
my father was French. We were raised on a sugar plantation,
where I spent most of my time surfing or working in the fields.
In those days no one surfed Pipeline, and so I had it all to
myself. It was a wonderful way to grow up—without a care in
the world.

When the Vietnam War came around I was drafted and
trained as a medic in the Green Berets. Most of the missions
were high risk and this particular one I didn't expect to return
from. The amazing thing is that President Johnson called back
the C-130 that I was on as it was in flight to Vietnam. None of
the men from my outfit who actually did go on this mission
survived. But by the grace of God, I was spared and soon found
myself back home in Hawai'i.

I first experienced Kalalau in 1967 when my friend and
I hiked in. No one lived there at the time but a philosopher
named Dr. Bernard Wheatley who lived in the big cave at the
west-end of the beach. They called him the Hermit of Kalalau.
When I arrived I was impressed at how immaculately clean
and swept his cave was. He looked up at me, smiled and said,

"Ya know I was going to leave a couple of days ago, but I had the feeling someone was going to come in." He enjoyed having company. We explored the valley together for several days.

The incredible thing about Kalalau is the stonework. They must have farmed every square inch of that place. We explored the archeological sites, and he showed me the secret places where the fruit grew up on the ridge.

Dr. Wheatley was a thoughtful man who seemed to have found a balance in nature, and I was fortunate to have had him as my guide. It was years after he left Kalalau that I began to see hunters and paniolo from the Robinson Ranch in the valley. They used to keep cattle there and that's what kept the trails clear. Now many of the old trails are choked with vines.

Anyway, you asked about the time I climbed out of Kalalau. I had been in there for a couple weeks and was living near the river mouth. It was beautiful—a place where I could watch the sunrise and sunset from a high plateau. One day another fellow and myself went deep into the valley in search of bamboo to build a geodesic dome. The next morning I was watching the sunrise from the ridge when I noticed these honeybees flying by and landing on the pīkake flowers. I could see they were flying to the other side of the valley. So I followed them.

The light was just right. You could see it glistening off their wings as they meandered up the valley. I followed them another couple hundred yards across the river and up to a big rock where I stood and listened. I could see where they kinda made a change of direction from up-valley and I followed them for another mile or so, until they disappeared into the hollow of a tree. Having experience from my plantation days, I had no trouble smoking them out and harvesting the honey.

When I returned with the honey, my friend and I gorged ourselves. It gave us a lot of energy and we followed the stream all the way to the back of Kalalau. When we finally got to the wall of the valley, we found a little goat trail that went underneath the ferns and we started crawling up this vertical incline.

There are other ways to climb out of Kalalau, but the way we went was to the back of the valley as far as we could go and straight up. We got a couple hundred feet up and looked back over Kalalau. It was really beautiful. We kept going up this ridge on our hands and knees until it got really narrow. It dropped straight off on both sides.

It was like being kids on an adventure...something to do and we were pumped. You chug a little of this real black, rich Kalalau honey and you're instantly energized. I had been in there for weeks resting and charging up my batteries and I was ready for action. Nature does that. It rejuvenates you.

The happiest times of my life have been in the valley just living there surviving on mango, oranges, and watercress soup. Fisherman would come in and throw their nets and they would be so full of moi that they could not tow them in...but that's another story.

We continued climbing up along the face of the cliffs, about a thousand feet, until we came to a little goat trail only a foot wide that formed the spine of a ridge. It was getting dark and I started crawling on my hands and knees. There was only a slim crescent moon and visibility was low. I remember hearing the roosters crowing as we were starting to get into the clouds. We were kind of feeling our way along this ridge when it dropped straight off on both sides. Eventually we got to a point where the trail disappeared altogether into a deep chasm. The Hawaiians, I think, had a name for it—Ka-leina-kaka (the struggling leap).

It was hard to tell how big the gap was, but by tossing rocks in front of us, we estimated it was about eight feet. We said, "God, should we try to jump across?" Then I saw an 'ōhi'a tree on the other side with all the roots exposed. We could jump for it and grab that root, but if we failed, it was straight down into the abyss. I jumped first and grabbed the root of the 'ōhi'a tree and pulled myself up. When my friend went he landed just above me. He caught hold of some ferns and when they came loose he started to slide down. I grabbed him with one arm and held the roots with the other, and then we pulled ourselves up. By then we were pretty cold and exhausted. All I had was a pair of shorts and a windbreaker. After crawling almost straight up through aluhi fern, we found a little pocket of dry ground and went to sleep wondering if we had passed the point of no return.

The next morning we woke to a beautiful sunrise and I said, "Well let's keep going." There is something about me that always wants to see new things. This was a new adventure and we were determined to go up and out. We had to climb through large thickets of Hawaiian raspberries on the way up and the thorns scratched every inch of my body. It just made me want to keep going. Actually we had no choice. We were on the side of the cliff hanging on. You can't rest or relax. You have to keep going. The raspberries we found along the way sustained us for the rest of the journey.

At about noon we made it to the top and found an old jeep trail and followed that a couple hundred yards to the Kōke'e lookout. Gazing 4,000 feet straight down to the base of Kalalau Valley I could only say: "Oh my God! We did it!"

Travelers' Nā Pali Tales

The many picturesque Nā Pali-focused Internet sites have impressive layouts, but they tend to either exaggerate the dangers of the trail, or ignore them entirely. Headings like "Red Cliffs of Death" are not uncommon, but it is more likely that the text refers to the challenges the writer faced getting the red clay stains out of her socks after a day-trip to Hanakāpī'ai Valley.

An interesting Web site where Nā Pali posts can be found is www.OutsideOnline.com. Readers are invited to rate a trip into Nā Pali as recommended, or not recommended. Two-thirds of the respondents had a positive response, while the other third would probably agree that the risk factor of Nā Pali far outweighs the thrill factor.

The comments culled from Outside Online represent an honest, if not accurate appraisal of what may be encountered on the Nā Pali. It is gorgeous…stunning…and jaw dropping, but it is also true that in places only a "few inches of loose dirt" may separate the hiker from the edge of a cliff; coastal streams do carry the deadly leptospirosis; and although the majority of people that you meet in Kalalau are friendly and hospitable, very strange people have been known to wander in the valleys.

You may well encounter heavy winds and rains, impassable streams, rock slides, overgrown trails, collapsing trails, disappearing trails, and extremely narrow trails bordering sheer cliffs. If you hike it often enough, eventually you can expect to experience all of these elements—let us hope that it does not happen to you all at once, as it has to some.

One popular novelist wrote, "You can hike the grueling eleven-mile trail, which deserves every decimal point of its Sierra Club rating: nine in difficulty on a scale of one to ten."

Most seasoned hikers would agree—Nā Pali is right up there with Cirith Ungol. But then again, there are hundreds of people a year who hike at least part of the trail and encounter no major difficulties other than the rigors of the trail itself. Everyone is naturally awed by the narrow passes, but they come to grips with the dangerous sections of the trail. Most hikers experience clear weather, mild streams, and relatively solid ground beneath their feet.

There are no guarantees, but a smart hiker gets an early start, goes in summer, and reads this book before taking the first step.

Outside Online—Trip Reports

"It was gorgeous...stunning...jaw dropping."

—Barbara

"The Kalalau Trail on the top half of the Nā Pali Coast is an absolutely incredible backpacking experience. A tough trail, 11 miles each way, leads through numerous, lush, hanging valleys to the spectacular Kalalau Valley and beach, a secluded Edenesque tropical paradise. The trip is not for those with vertigo or acrophobia as the trail hugs the sometimes precipitous slopes of the lava cliffs; at times only a few inches of loose, crumbly dirt is all that separates you from a fall into the incredibly clear, blue sea below. Despite the trouble getting there, Kalalau Valley is definitely worth the trip."

—Sage

Not recommended: "Although there were many breathtaking views along the trail, I believe one could appreciate the beautiful views from many other places on Kaua'i. If you have children do not go on the trail. Much of the trail is a sheer drop off on one side and is very steep. One of our fellow hikers nearly fell to her death. The water is extremely dangerous to swim in. This is not the trail for the average tourist hiker. I strongly advise anyone thinking of doing this hike to reconsider. There are many other, more pleasant activities to do on Kaua'i."

—Mark

Not recommended: "You have to be very fit to complete this trip. Yes, the beach at the end is amazing, but the people who live there in those caves will try to take you for everything. I hurt my leg and had to be rescued by a passing fishing boat by swimming out through killer surf. My friend had to walk out and collapsed half way, being rescued by passing campers."

"Not for the faint hearted. My worst nightmare come true. I was also bitten by a spider and ended up with a tennis ball-sized welt under my arm. Take plenty of water as the streams contain leptospirosis, which is deadly. Be prepared for some scary stuff if it is windy while you are out on the crumbling clay cliffs with sheer drop-offs on either side of you."

—Tracey

"It was a complete adventure. I started out with total confidence that I could pull this off because I recently had hiked the Inca trail in Machu Pichu and I was like…let's go! But it ended up being a lot harder than I thought it was going to be. Along the trail I realized it's not about endurance; it's about overcoming fear. And one of my greatest fears is height. I was hiking with my father and his good friend, Terry. I had just met Terry, so we didn't know each other that well, but on this trail you really get to know the people you are with. It is really interesting. When he fell, I fell at the same time and it was like, everything is so connected on the trail. He fell thirty feet. It was really bizarre. He was screaming 'I'm okay...I'm okay,' but really he wasn't. He ended upside down. It was a real mess. As soon as we hit the seven-mile mark the heights were really extreme. I was walking along imagining myself falling to my death, when I came to a place where the trail disappeared. I said, 'I can't do this.' Then I completely lost it. I screamed and started crying. Luckily Terry, who had just taken a death-defying fall, helped me across, but then he ended up falling again. I thought he was going to die and there is nothing I can do to help him. It was so intense. I was so shaken up I was crying pretty much the rest of the trail and thought I could never hike out."

—Tara Gladstone

I Crawled the Kalalau
By *Claudia Dawn Moeller*

September, 1981

A three-hour tour...sure. The plan was to drop off my husband's friend, Rick, at Kalalau Valley and be back in Hanalei by noon. After the first engine broke down a mile offshore, our skipper assured us that he had a backup. After the backup motor broke down a hundred yards off Kalalau Beach, he assured us that he could fix it.

An hour later, after his only pair of pliers broke in two, he confidently said, "If waves don't wash us ashore, the current will bring us to the island of Ni'ihau. But no worries, I know the Robinson family."

By then we were so pathetically seasick that our only concern was getting to dry land. With that we gave our best wishes to the skipper and promptly abandoned ship.

Rick, the fireman, had no experience in Hawaiian surf and while the rest of us managed to ride the waves in, he was caught in the impact zone and pummeled. When Sue saw that he was in a panic, she went back, grabbed hold of his arm and said, "You've got to swim. C'mon you big baby—now swim!"

They say the worst thing that can happen to a fireman, besides getting burned, is being called a "big baby." So Rick followed Sue's lead, caught a few waves and eventually made it to shore. On the beach we asked him what happened out there and all he could say was, "Incredible…it was like doing flips, cartwheels, and somersaults all at the same time!"

Meanwhile, the skipper finally succeeded in getting the engine started and signaled for us to swim back out to the boat. Sue shook her head and said, "There's no way I'm getting back in that boat." When I reminded her that it was past 1:30 p.m. and we still had a six or seven hour hike ahead of us, she uttered prophetically: "I'll take the Kalalau trail even if I have to crawl."

The choice between returning to Hanalei by boat in less than an hour as opposed to hiking barefoot for the next seven hours was a difficult decision to make. Would the motor break down again and leave us stranded against the face of the Nā Pali cliffs? If we hiked, would we make it to Kē'ē before sunset, or stumble off the cliffs in the dark?

Sue was determined to hike the trail, with or without us. We knew that we couldn't leave our dear friend behind, so my husband swam back out to the boat, gathered our shoes, and the three of us hit the trail.

We reckoned that without backpacks we could cut an hour or two off our time and be at Kē'ē Beach by sunset. By the time we reached the top of Red Hill it was obvious that this wasn't going to happen, but we were committed. The boat had already left and would be back in Hanalei by the time we reached the next ridge.

After vomiting all morning, rescuing a fireman from the surf, and climbing the steepest part of the trail, Sue was entirely spent. Yet in spite of the fact that her flip-flops had fallen apart, her feet were bleeding, and she was seeing double, she jogged with us all the way to Hanakoa Valley. There, beside the stream, she decided that she could go no further and insisted that we go on without her. I said, "Sue, you can't just curl up under a tree in the middle of nowhere. We have to stay together. Now let's go!"

For the next several hours as I began to suspect, I was dragging a corpse. Sue was hallucinating and so weak that by the time we reached Hanakāpīʻai, leaving her behind seemed like the only reasonable thing to do. At least she would be safe with the campers there. As we watched the sunset, I kept thinking, "Don't panic, only two more miles and we've reached the finish." Sue gathered her strength and forged ahead with us.

By the time we reached the top of the cutbacks, it was pitch black and pouring rain. My husband was the only one with a staff, so we clung to him, stumbling from rock to rock—a classic case of the blind leading the blind. The trail became so slippery and muddy that we finally came to a point where we could go no further, and so we started to crab-walk (face up and feet forward), never quite certain if we were on the trail or not. For the last half mile we slid from boulder to boulder until the final stretch, where gravity alone brought us to the head of the trail. What a wonderful sight!

Sue spent the next week in bed recuperating from that experience. At that time on Kauaʻi there was a popular T-shirt sold on the North Shore that read "I HIKED THE KALALAU 11." To cheer her up, I gave Sue a custom-made T-shirt that said, "I CRAWLED THE KALALAU 11."

We never realized what a profound effect this misadventure had on her until we received a letter from New Zealand several years later. It was Sue's testimonial of how her life was forever changed on the Kalalau Trail.

The Title Shot

On the return trip from Kalalau, I stopped near the seven-mile mark at Manono Ridge. It is aptly named Crawler's Ledge because on parts of the west side of this ridge there is an extremely narrow space between the cliff and a sheer drop-off. Most hikers who leave Kalalau at sunrise arrive at Manono a few hours later, and the only shady spot at that time of the day happens to be at this particular pass. Ahead is one of the steepest inclines of the trail with a series of cut-backs that provide no rest for the weary.

Naturally people want to stop at this place and some take the time to add their names to those written on the black lava cliffs.

As I sat in the shade gathering my strength for the climb ahead, I noticed the etchings on the cliff wall and decided to include the title of this book. However, as often is the case with graffiti, it soon became apparent that all the best places were taken.

Ten feet up and to the left was the suitable spot with a nice 2×3 foot flat space facing the trail. Without hesitation I picked up a piece of chalky white rock off the trail and climbed to within a few feet of the spot. It wasn't intimidating until I noticed that if I slipped at that point, I wouldn't be falling a few feet down to the trail, but straight off the face of the 400-foot cliff. After assessing the situation, I decided to go ahead and finish what I set out to do.

As I stretched out and wrote the first word, "Dramas," I lost my nerve. Slowly backing down the face of the cliff and seeing the lone word directly above me, I thought how ironic it would have been if I had fallen in the process of writing the title of this book. What became of me would surely have remained a mystery until my widow (who would have spent the rest of her days searching the citadels of Kalalau, and the glazed eyes of any passerby for clues of my whereabouts), saw the word "Dramas" written on the cliff above Crawler's Ledge and discovered my sun bleached bones on the rocks below.

Yet the dangling noun beckoned me. Would this be a lasting memorial to my fear of heights, or a tribute to all the brave souls who had found their way beyond these narrow passages and into the pages of this book?

I took a deep breath and climbed back up to the spot to complete the title. Afterward I looked up at "Dramas of Kalalau" on the face of the cliff, and I realized that my experiences have made me more than just a spectator, but a part of an ongoing saga that will continue as long as the Nā Pali stands above the sea.

Nā Pali Legends

Along with the art of hula and surfing, one of the greatest gifts that the Hawaiians have given the world is that of storytelling. They are masters of it. This tradition remains strong today as the ancient tales of night marchers, Menehune, and other mythical beings have become part of the fabric of modern day lore, particularly on Kaua'i where many of these stories originated.

I Saw the Night Marchers
By Gary Saldana, M.D., a practicing family physician on the North Shore of Kaua'i who has lived in Kalalau Valley

It had been raining for many days in Kalalau Valley. Night had fallen and I was just settling in when I heard them. At first I thought someone was playing a radio. The sound came from a distance, faint at first, and then it seemed to get closer and closer, a soft, hauntingly beautiful melody in a minor key.

I kept wondering who would be walking around the jungle in the middle of the night. It didn't make any sense. I didn't see any lights and as I waited the sounds kept getting clearer and I could hear the Hawaiian language in the melody. Then I saw an ethereal, glowing light, as it passed my tent. When it was barely ten yards away I could see other luminous shapes of people of various sizes all walking together. I didn't feel any fear. Maybe some, but it was more amazement.

I remembered the stories that I heard over the years of the Night Marchers and I always associated it with trouble. If you were in their path your life was in danger. But this seemed like a group that was just peacefully singing through the forest. As they moved on I didn't know what to think, other than the world is much stranger than it appears, and that our understanding of reality is limited. I remember the music lingered for a while then became a faint echo.

I tried to understand why it happened in Kalalau Valley, and why it did not occur in other places in the world. Who were these entities? Were they spirits, souls, or energies? Were they dead? Is there another universe that is as alive as ours is? What could they possibly represent? I suppose that any kind of conjecture or speculation is just that. Maybe one day a Hawaiian will be able to explain it to me. Until then I am left wondering.

The Night Marchers

It was a dark, stormy night when Ikaika and I took a shortcut over the heiau. Normally I would avoid a place like this for the same reason I would avoid walking over a graveyard at night. The question isn't why not, but why go there when it can be avoided? After all, didn't they used to make human sacrifices in this place? My friend didn't seem concerned, so I said nothing and followed him up the hill. Only after we were near the summit of the heiau did he bother to mention that "most Hawaiians would not even go near this place after dark."

"Why?" I asked, carefully avoiding contact with the boulders. As the flames of the candle reflected off his glasses, the tall Hawaiian said with a chilling stare…Ka huaka'i o ka Po, the Night Marchers. I didn't respond, but Ikaika could sense my uneasiness and said, "You no scared, eh?"

With all the aplomb of Barney Fife, I girded my loins (tugging on my lava lava) and said in a cocky Texas drawl, "Naugh, I ain't scared of no ghosts… but tell me more 'bout dem night crawlers."

Ikaika responded in a deadly serious tone.

"Eh, you no f--- with the Night Marchers! It's a procession of dead chiefs and warriors and gods. If you happen to be in their path and they cry 'kapu o moe'—you're a dead man."

This was Ikaika's story:

The march of the chiefs was accompanied by drums and nose flutes and other instruments, or silence except for the creaking of the calabashes and the mānele (litter) upon which the chief was carried. He would call an 'alo kapu, so that no man beast or bird could pass before him without being killed. In the march of the 'aumakua there was music and chanting as they passed. They carried candlenut torches (kukui) that burned brightly and were often followed by whirlwinds. When the procession passed by houses of the ali'i it might pause there and then pass. The family inside may not notice them, but a neighbor would see it pass and know that someone had died there.

The march of the gods was more brilliantly lit with red torches.

They walked six abreast with Hi'iakaikapoli o Pele, the younger sister of the volcano goddess, at the end. The only music to be heard was the chanting of their names and mighty deeds. The sign that accompanied them was a heavy downpour of rain or a mist. The next day their path would be strewn with broken boughs, for the heads of the gods were said to be sacred and nothing should be suspended above them. If there is a procession of chiefs and the victim has no time to get out of the way, then he must take off his clothes and lay face upward. He may hear them cry "shame" as they pass, but he should not even breathe. Another marcher might say, "He is dead," and another, "No he is alive, but what a shame for him to lie uncovered."

If there's not enough time to move then he should sit perfectly still, eyes closed. He may listen to them, but dare not look at them. It is likely that the guard at the front of the line will kill him unless he has an 'aumakua (ancestor) in the procession to plead for him. First he would hear the command "Strike!" then, if there was someone to intercede for him, he would hear, "No he is mine!" and only then perhaps he would be spared.

I interrupted Ikaika. "Have you ever actually seen these Night Marchers?" I asked.

"No, but my mother has," he replied. "On one occasion she felt something outside her door and then saw a strange mist penetrating the cracks."

"Hu!" I said, "The same thing happened to my wife!"

"What?"

"The mist."

"She didn't open the door, did she?"

"No. It was the window, our bedroom window. Why?"

"My mom opened it—big mistake. Eh, but what happened to you?"

I then told Ikaika what happened to my wife and me a few years back. It started early on a January morning. I left before dawn to build a memorial and to photograph the sunrise at Crater Hill along the coast at Kīlauea on Kaua'i's North Shore. About the time I approached the crater in Kīlauea something very strange occurred back home. My wife, who has never experienced anything of this sort before, was awakened and found she was terrified for no apparent reason. She felt an icy chill and said she saw an eerie mist pouring through the window. She started praying out loud. I'm not sure what was said, but knowing her low ghost tolerance, I can imagine that whatever it was immediately started to feel the heat and departed. She soon fell back asleep. Some Hawaiians might call this Ahu ka ʻalaʻala pula (a heap of relish made of octopus liver).

The plot thickened when my wife was re-awakened by the ringing of the phone. An old friend, Tom Hamilton, informed her that at sunrise he passed the entrance to Crater Hill and saw my car wrapped around a steel pole.

As I turned into the main entrance of Crater Hill that morning, one instant I was thinking of what a beautiful day it was and the next instant I was blinded by the morning light and struck a steel pole head on at 30 mph. As I sat there in a pool of blood trying to comprehend why anyone would place a pole in the middle of the road, the ambulance arrived. The driver said that by the looks of the car, he assumed I was dead. Actually I escaped with only a black eye and a few stitches.

When I returned from the hospital emergency room I found out the accident occurred at the same time that the mist had awakened my wife. "A heap of relish made of octopus liver," I thought.

The plot thickened again when a year later I met an elderly Hawaiian woman who had once owned the house we lived in, which was located along a ridge near Princeville overlooking Hanalei Bay. She had come back for a visit. As we strolled around the property reminiscing about Hurricane ʻIniki, I inquired about the concrete foundation that stood in the path between our bedroom window and Hanalei Plantation Road. What was it doing there? Her answer gave me chicken skin.

The foundation, she said, was exposed because the house it once supported had been moved. Her mother had lived there for many years, and often heard strange sounds in the night. It terrified her so much that she became ill and sent for a kahuna in hopes of removing the spirit. When the kahuna arrived he informed her that the path that the house was on lead to the ruins of the old Club Med property (located just above the Hanalei Pier on the Princeville side of the Hanalei River), which was built on Hawaiian ceremonial grounds. (The locals used to jokingly call it Club Dead because of all the ghost stories associated with the place.) "Your house," the kahuna said, "is on the path of the marchers."

The old woman cried: "My house sits on the path of the Night Marchers! Auwe! Now what am I to do?"

The kahuna then told her that if she wanted to sleep peacefully at night, she must leave, or move the house. At a cost of $10,000 she had the house moved ten feet to where it presently sits. The old concrete foundation is still there today.

I later moved into the house next door, which is located along the same trail. The good news is that it has an even better view. The bad news is that I'm right back in the middle of the trail. Auwe! I suppose that anyone who has seen the view of Hanalei Valley from this house would understand my reluctance to leave. Since then I haven't had any more bloody turf wars with the Night Marchers or their homies. No more freak accidents, strange sounds in the night, barns hurled at our bedroom wall, or eerie mists lingering about. This has led me to speculate that either I have become used to them, or they to me. It is not that they tiptoe past or anything, but things do seem to have settled down since I put up a "No Loitering" sign.

Naupaka

The ridge separating Pōhakuao Valley from Kalalau Valley is called Naupaka. The naupaka plant is a common beach shrub with jade-green leaves that grows on most Nā Pali beaches. There is also a mountain naupaka, which, like the beach variety, bears only a half bloom. There are slightly different versions of this particular legend of the Naupaka plant, but the essentials remain the same.

Legend has it that Chiefess Kilioe, the head of the hula school located above Kē'ē Beach at the Hā'ena end of the Kalalau Trail, was awakened one night by the sound of footsteps crossing a stream. None of her students were to be out at that hour of the night, and Kilioe sensed trouble.

This chiefess was no ordinary wahine, she was a mo'o, who could change into a reptile-like creature at will. Arming herself with her hardwood kauila staff she went to investigate the sound. Kilioe crossed the Limahuli Stream heading east, passing the spring of Waialoha, and stopping to search Maniniholo Cave (the dry cave at Hā'ena). She then continued over the Wainiha River along the path that leads to Lumaha'i Valley.

As the first rays of light passed over the sands of Naue, Kilioe saw two of her students coming around the point hand in hand. This angered her. Hula students' consorting was kapu, especially before graduation, when each student was commanded to remain "hidden from view."

Kilioe screamed out their names: "Nanau! Kapaka!"

When they saw her, the young lovers were terrified. "Hele!" cried Nanau. The couple fled down a hill and across a stream and ran down Lumaha'i Beach as fast as they could go. When they reached the rocks in the middle of the beach, Nanau told Kapaka: "Just ahead is Ho'ohila cave. Hide there. I will go to the mountains and Kilioe will follow me. When it is safe, I will return."

Kilioe followed the pair of footprints in the sand until they separated, then she heard Nanau on the cliffs just above her. She again screamed with rage and pursued him up the embankment. Suddenly, Kapaka came forth from the cave and confronted the mo'o.

"Stop!" she commanded.

Kapaka said, "Here I am, take me."

"Kapu breaker!" hissed the mo'o as she raised her staff and struck the young wahine in the head, killing her instantly. As the lifeblood of Kapaka sank into the sands of Lumaha'i, Kilioe turned to tracking down Nanau. She caught up with him high on a ridge known as Pu'uomanu, the Hill of the Birds, and there Kilioe slew Nanau. Like his beloved Kapaka, Nanau's lifeblood was spilt on the soil.

Satisfied that her students had been properly punished, Kilioe returned to the hula school above Kē'ē.

The following day she received alarming news. Fishermen reported that a strange plant, never before seen, had sprouted at Lumaha'i, and bird catchers at Pu'uomano reported the same plant now grew on that ridge.

Kilioe went to see for herself. On the beach where she had killed Kapaka, and in the mountains where she killed Nanau, she found a beautiful and new shrub that bore only a half flower. Today it is said that when the Naupaka kahakai (sea) flower and the Naupaka kuahiwi (mountain) flower are joined to form one beautiful blossom, then the two lovers, separated by death, will once again be reunited.

The Long Peace of Kamaluohua

Tradition has it that Kaluanuiohua, a powerful ali'i from the Big Island, had ambitions to conquer all of the Hawaiian Islands long before Kamehameha. To accomplish this he captured the ruling chiefs of Maui, Moloka'i and O'ahu. His conquest ended on Kaua'i where he was soundly defeated. The defeat gave Chief Kukona of Kaua'i a chance to be sovereign over all the islands.

The powerful chiefs, who had been brought with Kaluaniohua to Kaua'i, were now captives of Kukona. Rather than executing his prisoners and proclaiming himself king of all the islands, the Kaua'i ruler embarked with them on a tour of Nā Pali Coast, reckoning that a peace was preferable to further bloodshed.

One night as they camped at Lumaha'i Beach, Kukona pretended to fall asleep. As the prisoners huddled around the fire he overheard them plotting against him, saying, "Let us kill Kukona now and regain our freedom." But the chief of Maui replied: "We must do nothing to harm Kukona. Here we are prisoners in his hand and he has not put us to death."

Suddenly Kukona rose up pointing to the chief of Maui. Kukona said: "What a fine dream I have just had! I dreamed all of you were plotting my death but that one. He defended me and preserved my life."

The other chiefs acknowledged their guilt, and Kukona told them that he considered them far too untrustworthy to rule with him in a united Hawaiian kingdom.

With the exception of Kaluanuiohua, who was held for ransom, all the chiefs were freed after swearing that they, nor their descendents, would never again invade Kaua'i.

A tiny umu (shrine) of beach rocks built at Miloli'i, on the west end of Nā Pali, commemorates the oath sworn by the chiefs on the day that Kalailoaia Kamaluohua, "The Long Peace of Kamaluohua" began. The truce lasted until 1795 when Kamehameha began his conquest of all the Hawaiian Islands.

The Last of the Menehune

Hanakāpīʻai or Baysprinkling Food, was named after the Menehune Chiefess Hanakāpīʻai. She died in childbirth along Nā Pali as her people traveled toward Hāʻena on their way to their final departure from the shores of Kauaʻi. Historically, Menehune have been portrayed as colorful, romantic, mythical dwarves who accomplished magical feats of construction during the night. This, of course, is a fable. The flesh and blood Menehune were indeed a part of the Polynesian family with a large population settled on Nā Pali.

The existence of Menehune on Kauaʻi establishes an ancient connection with Central Polynesia not found on the other Hawaiian Islands. The subtle differences in language, the design of stone tools, the architecture of heiau, and the oral traditions found in Kauaʻi legends have been attributed to Menehune influence. One theory is that Tahitian voyagers, sailing to Kauaʻi from their home islands far to the south, gave the name Menehune to the aboriginal or first settlers of the island who likely migrated from Nuʻuhiwa or the Marqueses Islands, located to the northeast of Tahiti.

The Tahitians once proudly called themselves Manahune until they were conquered by Raiateans and the name was turned into a racial slur. Manahune came to mean "commoner." After they settled in Hawaiʻi, later migrations of Tahitians apparently did to their forebears as the Raiateans had done to them. This ancient Tahitian mele about the Manahune says a great deal about their social status in Southern Polynesia.

> Go to the mountains where you belong,
> Far, far away up there,
> Far away where the red skies lie,
> Away to the road of separation,
> Far away to the clustering yellow bamboos,

Torch-fisher of the nato of Motutu,
Picker of eels,
Thou art the grandchild of the mountain,
Thou slave of the Arii!

Because they were subjugated on Kaua'i as they had been in Tahiti, the Menehune people gathered at Wainiha to leave the island. After the deaths of Chiefesses Hanakāpī'ai and Hanakoa, their departure was delayed sixty days for a period of mourning. Tradition has it that there were twenty divisions of 6,000 men each and eight divisions of 20,000 women assembled at Wainiha as they sailed into the unknown.

In time, with a slight dialectical variation of the word Manahune, the name of the early settlers of Kaua'i became known as the Menehune. The myths about their size may have been influenced by the fact that they shared this island with Polynesians from Tahiti who, by any standard, were unusually large. It may also refer to their social status. Living under a system where "might is right," the Menehune could not compete.

To say that the Menehune built this fishpond or that terrace was perhaps to say that the "commoners" built it. Fanciful stories of their amazing building feats followed. The last written record of the Menehune is found in a 1800s missionary census taken on Kaua'i in which sixty-five persons described their heritage as Menehune.

According to another tradition, 500,000 Menehune once dwelt on Kaua'i. Their king was upset at the number of marriages between Menehune and Hawaiians, so he assembled them and began preparations for a great departure to an undisclosed destination. Only Mohikia asked if he could remain behind with his Hawaiian wife. The chief granted his request and with the exception of a few families that hid out during the departure from Wainiha, all the Menehune left Kaua'i forever.

In the Kaua'i census sixty-five Menehune were recorded living at the head of Wainiha Valley, close to Mount Wai'ale'ale, in a community known as La'au.

Some Hawaiians dispute this claim and insist that the folk were Mu, not Menehune. Others have said that although they were close relatives, one could tell the difference between a Mu and a Menehune by the shape of their abdomens. They were also distinguished by what they carried, with Menehune holding rocks, while the Mu held bananas. At that time Menehune were said to affectionately refer to the Mu children as, "banana eating bugs." This may seem irrelevant until you make the mistake of referring to a rock-carrying Menehune as a Mu. Although they were not very big, you would not want to get on the bad side of a Menehune. They may be depicted in tourist's guides as cute little do-gooders, but if provoked, they could be fierce warriors.

The Menehune tribe living on the island of O'ahu was last heard from in AD 1700. About that time Chief Kuali'i was having a difficult time rooting them out of their stronghold in Mānoa Valley above Waikīkī. This was a major embarrassment to him. The chief is lauded in Hawaiian chants as master of the land, sea, sun, stars, and rain—but he could not master the Menehune. Being unable to rid his island of a sworn enemy brought the mana (power) of the chief into question.

When Kuali'i learned that Menehune were terrified of pueo, the Hawaiian owl, he imported hundreds of them from Kaua'i to scare his unwanted guests away.

Apparently the Kaua'i pueo were more experienced at taunting the Menehune. They hunted at night when, according to legend, Menehune did their work. The pueo also held a symbolic significance and were regarded by the Hawaiians as spiritual guardians who protected and guided them in the night. After being released over Mānoa Valley, the army of hungry pueo struck terror into the ranks of the Menehune, and gave confidence to their enemy. Their Menehune chief finally surrendered and led his people away from O'ahu forever.

Besides the Menehune and the Mu, Hawaiian mythology has other mysterious figures of the night including the Wa and the Wao. Deeper in the forest were the Nawa (noisy beings), Namu (silent beings) and all manner of disgruntled, misshapen, and otherwise impish characters who were lumped under the term 'e'epa.

If someone said something strange, the response might be, Ho'i i Wainiha i Kahi o ka 'e'epa. (go to Wainiha where the supernatural beings dwell). In other words, go be with your own kind.

The Last Kalalau Settlers
By Michael Olanolan of Wainiha

Michael Olanolan's ancestors, the Maka family, were originally from the island of Ni'ihau and moved to Kalalau Valley before Hawai'i became a United States Territory in 1900. The Olanolans are from Wainiha, the Dodge City of one-horse towns on the North Shore of Kaua'i, and operate the old Wainiha Store on the road to the Kalalau Trail.

My grandfather Jacob Maka was born in Kalalau. He was a taro farmer. That's about all there was to do back there. From what I understand, the Makas were among the last families in Kalalau, along with the Mahuikis and the Pa family. Everyone was forced out of Kalalau when they had that leprosy thing going on in there. The government army at the time was trying to capture Ko'olau and anyone in the valley who did not have leprosy was taken away by boat and dropped off in Hā'ena. Those with leprosy were taken on to the leper colony at Kalawao (on Moloka'i). Grandpa Maka did well on the outside and became a successful entertainer, composer, and politician on Kaua'i.

When I was a kid I used to go into Kalalau on a Friday after school and come home on Sunday. Whenever I told my dad I was going to go hunting, he would never say no, because it was for food. They never had pig back then, only goat. I would ride a horse all the way in. The trail was much better in those days.

I haven't been in Kalalau for many years because the last time I was there I was fined for not having tags for the goats that I killed. I had a hunting permit, but I forgot my tags on the boat. The game warden gave me a ticket and they ended up taking away my rifle and hunting license for a year. At the time I wasn't aware of my native gathering rights. My family is from Kalalau. I had a right to be there, but did they?

Today Kalalau is not well taken care of—not the way it used to be. It's not just the people that are in there today; this has been going on for decades. They use the trail a lot less than they did in the old days when they had cattle running in and out of there.

In the wintertime when the sea was rough, it was hard to go by canoe to Hāʻena, so the Hawaiians would walk the 11-mile Nā Pali Trail. In the summer they would canoe up and down the coast. It was easier and faster. But nowadays people walk off of the trail to avoid the mud. Eventually the vegetation gets eroded away. Once you kill the plant, the root is gone, and the dirt runs off.

The same thing has happened in Kalalau. In the old days there used to be all guava trees and plum trees along the beach, but the people living there cut most of the trees down for firewood— wiped them out. They cut the tree, it dies, the root dies, and there is nothing to hold the ground. Eventually it all erodes away.

When I was in eighth grade I worked with the state Job Corp for wayward kids and they put me to work on the Nā Pali Trail. I used my mule to carry in bags of cement—four at a time. All the places that you see cement reinforcing the trail—that was our work.

My family has lived on the North Shore for generations, but we all remember our roots in Kalalau with pride.

Kalalau Paniolo

No book about Kalalau would be complete without reference to Samson Mahuiki, a friendly, wise elderly Hawaiian man from Hāʻena who was once a Kalalau paniolo. Over the past century-and-a-half his family migrated from the Forbidden Island of Niʻihau to Kalalau Valley, and then to Hanalei where Samson served as the fire chief for the North Shore and Nā Pali Coast. Following is Samson's account of his life and times in Kalalau and on the Kalalau Trail.

I had about twenty-five head of cattle in Kalalau that I drove from Hanakāpīʻai. I worked alone with whatever dogs I get. They were three not specially trained, but they knew how to chase. So I used them for every thing from hunting pig and goat, to rounding up cattle.

The trail was no problem. I held the cattle up at the head of the trail, then I brought in my tame horse and turned him loose to go to Hanakāpīʻai. After that I would release the cattle one by one and follow behind them. The horse knew the trail, and with the cattle in the back, he would go forward and the cattle would follow the scent.

In the valley it was no problem, with good feed they would stay there. The first time I put them on the trail to Hanakāpīʻai six went missing. I assumed that they had fallen off the trail, but they went up-valley Hanakāpīʻai and lived for a couple years. I found them when Kaipo and I had a contract to put up mile markers on the trail.

My family had a good stallion that was our car. In 1946 he broke his rope and my dad gave him a year off so he could roam with the herd. But every time we needed him, he would pass slow and easy. Most of the time he ran loose in Hā'ena. He did not act like most horses, you know, run here, run there. He never knew where he was going, so he didn't have to hurry.

After my mom's mare died we began to see wild horses in Kalalau, so every time we were there we would try to get one for her. We came close to one with a noose that we set on the trail, but never did catch it. It was easier in Hā'ena. A lot of people who had horses there freed them before they moved out. No one knew it at the time, but I would catch them. I would tie them up to a tree and tie a string around their lip. The next day when their mouth was all tender, they were easy to lead. I would take them to the beach and break them in the water. If they headed for the trees, I bailed out.

On horseback there was only one dangerous place on the trail—right after Hanakāpī'ai at the top of the zigzag. It's not hazardous to man, but you may lose your horse there. It's on a slope crossing a large, flat stone, so you don't want to make a mistake. We would go across there with one foot out of the stirrup. A couple of horses fell down to the ocean.

I used to like to take one green horse to Kalalau cause they don't care what they are doing. They are going to kick, buck, and bite, so well...the trail will take that all out. It's like a guy walking who is out of shape. Too bad, he's going to be crying—we treat the green horses that way.

When I had a group with me I would put the least experienced rider in front so they don't see how bad it is. When you are climbing over the stones and you hunch your back, the back of the saddle separates up la dat, and the greenhorns see it and say, "I'm going home." So they jam the whole thing up. Nobody wants to go back once they have gone that far, and already loaded up their horse. That's why I say to everybody, "If you can ride, you can go with me. If you want to walk, well…"

As the fire chief I tried to utilize the talent of each man. For Kalalau rescues, that's mine. Even the ocean, the best waterman, he is the guy that steps forward. We asked the guys, whatever you do best, you take 'em. In rescues along the Nā Pali I could do better on a horse than four guys walking in, who would have to carry the body out.

We never had, da kine, "fool around time." The sun doesn't wait for you. Any rescue on the Pali, I would ask, "What is the nature? Tell me where." Then I go. If the victims were traumatized, I would put them on a horse and say, "Squeeze that pommel small." And if they didn't ride a horse, they will get on a horse. This was the fastest way since a helicopter can not go everywhere. There were landing zones at Kalalau, Hanakoa, and Hanakāpī'ai, but from there the men would have to hike in on foot and then carry the victim all the way back.

As kids, we never slept on the trail. Even up till not to long ago people tell me they experience these Night Marchers even at camp Naue in Hā'ena. Guys like you even had that experience. My uncles, who lived in Kalalau, always told us stories that gave us chicken skin. They knew because they could hear the sound of the walking cane on the floor as it passed through that house. You know, right on Kalalau flat going toward the stream. When we used to go there, it still had the foundation. Best off don't sleep there. I would sleep by the mouth of the stream underneath the big mango tree. There are still some graves there, but that was about the safest place.

My mom always told us, "No, you have the spirit of the Lord now, you know who Jesus is…ahhhh, you can go anywhere." She said the same thing to [kumu hula Roselle] Baily who was scared to open up the ancient hula halau at Kē'ē.

After the provisional army ran the lepers out of Kalalau [in 1893], there were very few people left. There were all sorts of rumors, but I knew. My dad told me stories about the families in Kalalau. There was Hanohano Pa, the Maka family, my uncle Kalei, and a few others.

They used to take two horses on the trail into Kalalau. If you were going to stay the night you would use them both in order to take stuff in and out. When you arrive you pack the Kalalau supplies on the extra horse and then let it go. It knows where it's from, and it's gonna go home.

As a child I did the trail barefoot. We never had money for buy shoes. In those days nobody had money. That was only for the guys in Honolulu who needed them.

We used to go to Hanakoa every December to gather oranges for Christmas. It was our Foodland. But the best time to gather them is in spring when they are ripe and sweet! Even now when I look at the young haoles who live around here and they go barefoot, I look at their feet and feel the pain.

Kalalau Poems

<u>Ka Noe—The Mist</u>

In dreams I've seen the valley rising out of the mist
like an emerald set upon a silver band
The earth fell away in the shadow of clouds and over the falls
of Kalalau the white water roared…
Through the jungle it chiseled my dream
cut deep in the lava—under the stream
into the ocean where all streams end
then up to the heavens and back again

Ma ka moe 'uhane au
i 'ike ai ke Kalalau
e puka mai ana mai
ka noe mai me he
emelala

—Terence James Moeller 2001

<u>In Visions</u>

In visions I have seen the ancient citadels,
its spires of gold ablaze in azure sky,
glistening like swords raised for battle
None would dare assail her great walls or
flank her buttressed beauty
A queen art thou, oh Kalalau,
yet who first furled thy banner
and raised thy skirts to gaze upon this mystery?

—Kona Lowell 2000

Kalalau Dawn

Soft as the moonlight over Hanalei
casting shadows on a silver sea
Faint as a whisper are the wings of dawn
passing o'er the pale moon
at twilight in Kalalau
A crimson orb beneath the bough
"and thou, beside me in the wilderness."
—Terence James Moeller 2005

Useless Beauty

His name was writ in water that
lapped upon the shore
The sound of it was qssshhhhhh,
though I wasn't really sure
I asked the geese who know these things,
who wrought this paradise?
The nene only flew away toward the western sky
Behold, I said, a masterpiece…a symphony of flight
The artist has his signature on everything in sight
A love of useless—boundless—breathless beauty,
purple neon fish in the depths of the sea,
quasars exploding light years away,
a trillion miles of empty space with
orchids at my feet
Triple rainbows appear though one is excess
Dolphins leap to see the sunset
This useless beauty was all too much for me
I shut my eyes and turned away,
said that it was vanity,
a wasteful inefficient use of space
Then slept another sleepless night and
dreamt in worlds of black and white

No ginger laden waterfalls, or tropic birds that sing
In fact there was no life at all running
through these veins
You call this art? I cried aloud
An echo answered back
Then said the potter to the clay…art is more than that
Art is for the living, though dead men
try in vain to understand the mystery of
what I do each day
Bounds were placed upon the earth and set upon the sea
but none were placed upon your heart to hold eternity
Beauty reigns to fill the void and elevate the soul
That restless steed with wings of fire is rearing now to go
—Terence James Moeller 2004

Kalalau Reader

Hollywood and Kalalau
By Chris Cook

Hollywood location filming at Kalalau and along other
Nā Pali valleys has been limited compared to the extensive
use of Kaua'i in over forty feature films.

In the 1976 movie version of *King Kong*, Paramount Pictures
and Dino De Laurentiis recreated the Valley of Kong at Kalalau
and Honopū, which is the best known site. The uninhabited,
towering pinnacles and jungle-covered landscape of the Nā
Pali valleys and their relatively close proximity to civilization
made the locations ideal.

Actors and filmmakers flew in daily from the Princeville
Resort aboard chartered helicopters. Noticeable by his absence
was King Kong, who remained on a back lot in Hollywood
during the filming except for a huge paw print dug out of a
sea cliff just east of Kalalau Valley.

Two tons of filming equipment were shipped to Kaua'i,
including a small boat sent from Hollywood to match studio
shots with Nā Pali scenes.

The Kaua'i footage simulates the arrival of an exploratory
crew who row in from an oil company research vessel to the
white-sand shores of a cloud-covered, mysterious island said
to be somewhere off the north coast of Java. There, at Kalalau
Valley, they discover a towering, carved wooden wall that
protects islanders from the wrath of a huge beast. Jessica
Lange, in her screen debut recreating Fay Wray's famous
heroine role from the first Kong film, has been rescued at sea
by the research vessel, only to be captured by island natives

and offered as a sacrifice to Kong. The oil company crew strikes into the hidden Valley—set at Honopū—to rescue Lange.

Remote communications for the location filming in this pre-cellular phone era were handled by using a radio transmitter set up at the hotel.

The producers were on a tight schedule, with a Christmas opening in 1,000 US theaters already promised. De Laurentiis sent his 21-year-old son Fredrico to be the Kaua'i location producer. Filming at the remote Nā Pali locations provided the biggest challenge. Every day actors and crew members, food, and filming gear had to be flown in to the valleys by helicopter.

During the boat-landing scene at Honopū, larger-than-normal summertime surf caused problems. Kaua'i actor Wil Welsh, done up with fake sideburns, doubled on camera for actor Charles Grodin in long shots of the landing scene.

Special effects on-site were minimal, limited to technicians creating a morning fog with aerosol canisters near the Honopū arch. Footage taken within Kalalau Valley is overlaid with the studio-created Kong's Valley wall in the finished film.

Greg MacGillivray of MacGillivray Freeman Films of Laguna Beach, California used shots of a hang glider soaring down to Kalalau Beach in his pioneering IMAX film *To Fly* released in 1976 to mark the American Bicentennial, with a world premiere at the Smithsonian Institution's Aerospace Museum in Washington, D.C. The incredible scene filmed above Kalalau shows a hang glider soaring within close range of towering pinnacles over a thousand feet above Nā Pali valleys using a bird's-eye-view point of view.

MacGillivray returned in the early 1980s to film *Behold Hawai'i*, a mythical story of a young Hawaiian boy who goes back in time on Kaua'i to the days of ancient Hawai'i. A key scene features kahuna and ali'i gathered at Kalalau Lookout for the annual makahiki procession.

More recently, Harrison Ford and Anne Heche played a plane-wrecked couple on Nā Pali in *Six Days/Seven Nights* filmed in the late 1990s. The US Navy's Barking Sands commander assisted the film crew with logistical support for the remote location filming.

While Ford didn't appear in these scenes, director Steven Spielberg sent a second unit crew out to Kalalau for brief takes of local extras dressed as South American Indians leading pack animals in *Raiders of the Lost Ark*.

A little-known sci-fi film titled *Millennium* employs the Red Hill section of the Kalalau Trail.

Nā Pali in the 1800s
By Chris Cook

Nā Pali for tourists in the 1890s

For twenty miles along the northwestern coast of Kaua'i there extends a series of ridges, none less than 800 feet high, and many nearly 1,500 feet, terminating in a bluff that is unrivalled in majesty. Except for a very narrow, dangerous foot-path, with yawning abysses on each side, this bluff is impassable. Innumerable streams, forming wonderful cascades as they leap hundreds of feet in their tempestuous decent, pour over this bluff in the rainy season, and become mist before they reach the ocean. Beyond the raging surge, unbroken by any protecting reef, dashes against the precipitous walls of rock. *The Mikahala* on her circuit trips sails within 400 yards of these palisades, which are interrupted only by an ancient retreat of the chiefs at Milolii, with its fortified fish pond and impregnable valley, accessible from the land only by a pole ladder.

—Henry Whitney in the first tourist
guide to Hawai'i, c. 1890

Whitney was the son of pioneer Waimea missionary Samuel Whitney, and the founder of the *Pacific Commercial Advertiser*, the forerunner to today's *Honolulu Advertiser*.

Missionary Hiram Bingham toured Nā Pali aboard a double-hull outrigger canoe in the summer of 1821.

Unlike author James Michener's stereotyping of Protestant American missionaries as hard-nosed, uninterested in the Hawaiian culture Calvinists sent to the Sandwich Islands in the 1820s, missionary leader Hiram Bingham was an adventurer. He crossed Nā Pali in the summer of 1821, sketching the ladder at Nu'alolo and thoroughly enjoying himself. Following is his account first published in 1822, and later included in his autobiography.

The next morning, the kings started on their way eastward, and we returned by double canoe, around the north-western end of the island, where the mountains are very bold, some rising abruptly from the ocean. At one place, the pointed and lofty peaks, and sharp ridges and spurs, are cast in fantastic forms, and being crowded together, resemble in their sharpness and closeness, the lobes of honey-comb in an upturned bee-hive. At another part of this precipitous coast, we landed where there is a small tract of sterile ground, partly environed by a stupendous precipice, nearly perpendicular, forming at its base a semicircular curve which meets the ocean at each end. This vast rock rises at the ends of the curve about 300 feet, and in the centre nearly 2500 feet.

Commencing the ascent by a rude ladder that hangs over the sea, natives sometimes climb for amusement to the summit, to exhibit their simple fire-works, and throw off torches, so constructed, that they will reach the sea. Near one end of the curve, the rough face of the rock projects gradually forward some fifty feet, so as to cover a little hamlet built under its shelter, where the frail houses of the poor inhabitants are generally defended from the rain, and always from the direct rays of the sun, till afternoon. The cool shade of this rock, at half-past ten, in mid-summer, extended more than one hundred feet from its base.

Never was I so impressed by any natural scenery with the forcible figure by which Isaiah sets forth the Messiah as "a hiding-place from the wind and a covert from the storm,—the shadow of a great rock, in a wary land."

Near this settlement, a party of natives — men, women and children, were engaged in fishing in a singular manner still in vogue. Diving down, they place among the stones a native plant—the auhuhu called a poison, which appears to intoxicate the fish. The natives then dive or swim after them, and take them in their hands, or sitting in canoes, or standing near the shore, take them easily in scoop nets.

It was amusing to see our attendants, as we passed along, join in the sport, diving off from our double canoe, first on one side, and then on the other, and seizing the bewildered fish, turned on the side, swimming near the surface, and struggling in vain, like the inebriate, to avoid the destroyer.

—From "A Residence of Twenty-One Years in the Sandwich Islands" by Hiram Bingham

Backdoor Kalalau Adventures
By Chris Cook

The *Garden Island* newspaper archives hold at least a half dozen tales of successful, and unsuccessful, attempts at climbing down from the Alaka'i Swamp—Kōke'e upland to Kalalau Beach.

In recent years plant researchers sponsored by the National Botanical Garden at Lawa'i safely repelled down.

Other climbs have ended in tragedy, with deaths and serious injuries.

Following World War II, into the early 1950s, veterans still seeking adventure turned to the Kalalau descent.

In the summer of 1962 Bataan Death March survivor Bill Joy of Honolulu, writer Eugene Ressencourt, and Kalihi High School student Henry Kam made the descent, and described it in detail. Joy employed his surveying skills and preplanned the descent. His fall line was illustrated across a series of three snap shots.

"We did it to prove it could be done—and to be able to say we had done it," Ressencourt wrote.

The trio followed up with a paddle to Nu'alolo on air canvas air mattresses, and a hike to Hā'ena along the Kalalau Trail.

Another early 1960s climber, a German-born sailor and experienced mountaineer broke his leg trying to reach the Kalalau Lookout from below. The hiker was found by Dr. Bernard Wheatley, the Hermit of Kalalau.

Below is an account of a successful ascent made in 1924 from the *Garden Island* newspaper July 1, 1924.

Kalalau Pali Climbed by Boys

Four Kauai high school boys have the record of being the first to scale the Pali from Kalalau to Kōke'e. The feat was accomplished last Friday by Ernie and Edward Cheatham, Frank Thomas and James Hogg.

The four boys had gone into Kalalau from Hā'ena on Saturday, June 21. They spent several days hunting in the valley and when it came to start for home, decided to make the attempt to climb out to Kōke'e.

They broke camp a day early in case they were not able to make the climb so as to go out by Hā'ena if they failed to reach Kōke'e.

According to Kamaainas this is the first time that anyone has climbed out of the valley since the time of Ko'olau. Formerly there was a good trail in the valley from Kōke'e, but shortly after the reign of Ko'olau the trail was washed out and it was said to be impossible to make the trip either way.

The climb of four thousand feet took the party all day and several times they were forced to change their plans and make a different assault due to the fact that they found a spot that looked apparently easy was through brush although a good portion of it was in the open. The boys state that the climbing through the brush, although more uncomfortable, was considerably easier than the scaling of the palis in the open.

There was one or two near-tragedies, both being due to climbers being struck by rocks loosened by their comrades above them. Fortunately in both cases the boys were able to keep their holds although stunned by the rocks.

The top was finally gained in the evening and the boys were so exhausted that no attempt was made to go to Kōke'e but camp was made at the top. They hiked into Kōke'e the next morning and were fortunate in securing a ride to Waimea on the Hofgaard truck. From Waimea they were given a lift home by friends.

The boys say it is a great experience but they have no desire to make it again. They will rest on their laurels and will let some(one) else make any other attempts.

The Hermit of Kalalau
By Chris Cook

Dr. Bernard Wheatley of the Virgin Islands lived in what was then known as Hermit's Cave along Kalalau Beach from 1957 into the late 1960s.

His home was paved in part with smooth river stones, and encompassed an area 100 yards long by 40 yards deep, with a ceiling sloping down from 60 feet to 12 feet.

Wheatley served in the US Army during World War II as a physician, lived in Sweden for a while, but turned his back on the world for Kalalau in 1957 following the death of his wife.

In a *Honolulu Star-Bulletin* newspaper article by Eugene Ressencourt, published in August 1962, Wheatley was described as a man of African descent who went to top schools in Europe and America, as an athlete and successful doctor.

As Ressencourt approached Wheatley on the beach at Kalalau he stuck out his hand and said, "Dr. Wheatley, I presume," echoing Stanley finding Livingstone in Africa.

"...this modern messiah then chose at a certain time in his young life to 'give away,' as the Bible inspires, his 'worldly possessions' and to search at length his soul," Ressencourt reported.

"I do not intend," Wheatley told the reporter, "to live in this cave forever; but a man has a right to privacy, I think, and at present I do not want to be talking with people or engaging in activities."

Wheatley's living quarters were furnished with an air mattress, a lava rock stove, a selection of recent magazines, and a safe of sorts located overhead on a ledge inside his cave. His kitchen was immaculate, with silverware and china settings.

The "Hermit" meticulously combed the sand inside his cave with a yard-long board to remove footprints and keep it neat, and warned the reporter not to swim off Kalalau.

Wheatley was busy writing, Ressencourt noticed, and had recently completed a manuscript titled *A Primer for the Atomic Age*.

Period photos show Wheatley in top shape from a diet of fruit and vegetables and regular hiking in Kalalau, and out to Hanalei for supplies.

The arrival of hippie campers in the late 1960s drove Wheatley out, and he later lived in the Wailua area, where he died in 1991 at the age of seventy-two.

Plans announced in his death notice in the *Honolulu Advertiser* newspaper included the spreading of his ashes in the ocean off Kalalau Beach.

Jack London and Kalalau
By Chris Cook

Jack London and his wife, Charmain, sailed into Pearl Harbor in the spring of 1907 aboard their yacht the *Snark*.

Accompanying the couple on the long sail that began in Oakland, California, was Herbert Stolz, the son of Waimea Deputy Sheriff Louis Stolz. The elder Stolz was shot and killed in Kalalau Valley by the legendary Westside paniolo Kaluaiko'olau, the man London's fictional story *Koolau the Leper* is based on. Stolz apparently told London his family's side of the shooting of their father during their California to Hawai'i voyage.

Koolau the Leper first appeared in 1909 in the magazine *Pacific Monthly*, and became London's best known Hawai'i-set short story after the publication of *The House of Pride*, a collection of his Hawai'i stories.

London visited Kaua'i in May 1915 as a guest of a congressional party touring the island. He enjoyed a lū'au near Niumalu thrown by Nawiliwili businessman Jack Coney and boarded with the family of the Rev. John Lydgate. He drove from Lihu'e to Hanalei to board a steamer back to Honolulu.

His driver was Walter Sanborn of Hanalei, and the two men discussed details of the Ko'olau story, according to Sanborn's account of the ride in the papers of the Kaua'i Historical Society.

London used Ko'olau as a personification of the problems facing native Hawaiians following the overthrow of the Hawaiian Kingdom in 1893, and, though he never traveled to Kalalau, used the valley as a backdrop to his story. Following is an excerpt from London's *Koolau the Leper*.

And over these things Koolau was king. And this was his kingdom—a flower-throttled gorge, with beetling cliffs and crags, from which floated the blattings of wild goats. On three sides the grim walls rose, festooned in fantastic draperies of tropic vegetation and pierced by cave entrances—the rocky lairs of Koolau's subjects. On the fourth side the earth fell away into a tremendous abyss, and, far below, could be seen the summits of lesser peaks and crags, at whose bases foamed and rumbled the Pacific surge. In fine weather a boat could land on the rocky beach that marked the entrance of Kalalau Valley, but the weather must be very fine. And a cool-headed mountaineer might climb from the beach to the head of Kalalau Valley, to this pocket among the peaks where Koolau ruled; but such a mountaineer must be very cool of head, and he must know the wild-goat trails as well. The marvel was that this mass of human wreckage constituted Koolau's people should have been able to drag its helpless misery over the giddy goat trails to this inaccessible spot.

"Brothers," Koolau began.

But one of the mowing, apelike travesties emitted a wild shriek of madness, and Koolau waited while the shrill cachinnation was tossed back and forth among the rocky walls and echoed distantly through the pulseless night.

"Brothers, is it not strange? Ours was the land, and behold, the land is not ours. What did these preachers of the word of God and the word of Rum give us for the land? Have you received one dollar, as much as one dollar, any one of you, for the land? Yet it is theirs, and in return they tell us we can go to work on the land, their land, and that what we produce by our toil shall be theirs. Yet in the old days we did not have to work. Also when we are sick, they take away our freedom."

"Who brought the sickness, Koolau?" demanded Kiloliana, a lean and wiry man with a face so like a laughing faun's that one might expect to see the cloven hoofs under him. They were cloven, it was true, but the cleavages were great ulcers and livid putrefactions. Yet this was Kiloliana, the most daring climber of them all, the man who knew every goat trail and who had led Koolau and his wretched followers into the recesses of Kalalau.

"Ay, well questioned," Koolau answered. "Because we would not work the miles of sugar cane where once our horses pastured, they brought the Chinese slaves from overseas. And with them came the Chinese sickness—that which we suffer from and because of which they would imprison us on Molokai. We were born on Kauai. We have been to the other islands, some here and some there, to Oahu, to Maui, to Hawai'i, to Honolulu. Yet always did we come back to Kauai. Why did we cowl back? There must be a reason. Because we love Kauai. We were born here. Here we have lived. And here shall we die—unless—unless—there be weak hearts among us. Such we do not want. They are fit for Molokai. And if there be such, let them not remain. Tomorrow the soldiers land on the shore.

Let the weak hearts go down to them. They will be sent swiftly to Molokai. As for us, we shall stay and fight. But know that we will not die. We have rifles. You know the narrow trails where I must creep, one by one. I, alone, Koolau, who was once a cowboy on Niihau, can hold the trail against a thousand men. Here is Kapahei, who was once a judge over men and a man with honor, but who is now a hunted rat, like you and me. Hear him. He is wise."

Kayaking Nā Pali
By Chris Cook

Kayaking Nā Pali is a popular summertime activity, and an alternative to hiking the Kalalau Trail to camp in Kalalau Valley.

Conditions are generally safe from Memorial Day through Labor Day, according to guidelines posted online by the state Department of Land and Natural Resources. However, gusty trade winds and small north swells can come up at anytime during the summer.

Kayakers launch at Hāʻena and take advantage of the westward flowing coastal current and trade winds that blow from the northeast to make their way down the coast about fifteen miles to the state park at Polihale. Polihale is the northern tip of the twenty-mile-long Barking Sands beach on the island's Westside. It is advisable to secure a pickup at Polihale to drive you back to the North Shore or other location on the island.

Kayak camping permits are required to stay overnight at Kalalau or Miloliʻi, the two designated state camping grounds on Nā Pali for kayakers. Permits should be acquired well in advance of a trip. For visitors, it is advisable to book a guided tour with one of the other kayak tour companies located on the island.

The pluses of kayaking versus hiking Nā Pali are seeing the coast from a different viewpoint, most likely a faster trip due to the direct route and aid from the trade winds, the ability to pack in more equipment, and access to valleys beyond Kalalau.

The negatives of a Nā Pali kayak journey are seasick-ness and the potential for dangerous surf landings.

Kayakers should be in good shape and good swimmers, and have had some kayaking paddling experience and a knowledge of ocean safety.

Contacts:

Kayak camping permits
www.Hawaii.gov/dlnr/dsp/NaPali/kayak.htm

Guided kayak tours
www.kayakkauai.com
www.outfitterskauai.com

The Legend of Ko'olau the Leper

*And Waimakemake, with your sheltering foliage which hid us
and sheltered us from death, from the bullets of the raging ones, you
are the witness of the unerring aim of the daring hero in your bosom,
of our thirst and our hunger, you cherished and hid us, remembrance
of you is a fragrant garland, burnt and bound into this heart—for in
you is my steadfast love until my bones are laid away.*

—From the "Memoirs of Pi'ilani"

Kalalau Stream's main tributary flows down Waima-kemake Falls, a picturesque waterfall tucked away a few thousand feet up on the northeast rim of the valley. Access is via an ancient trail restored by Boy Scouts in 1982 following the devastation of Hurricane 'Iwa. Today it is once again overgrown.

Waimakemake is the setting for a famous story that has come to symbolize the decade in the late 1800s when the Hawaiian Kingdom was overthrown and Hawai'i became a territory of the United States.

It was from these jagged cliffs of Kalalau Valley in 1893 that the legendary Kaluaiko'olau more commonly known today as Ko'olau the Leper, faced off troops from the Provisional Government of Hawai'i sent to capture him.

The mission of the troops sent by steamer from Honolulu, to capture Ko'olau and take him to the isolated Kalalau leper colony at Kalawao on Moloka'i's North Shore.

Ko'olau and his family had joined a colony of lepers at Kalalau who resisted orders to be exiled from Kaua'i to Moloka'i. Most camped near the beach at Kalalau, while Ko'olau and his family sought refuge deeper in the valley.

Because his wife Pi'ilani wasn't allowed to join him on Moloka'i as her husband's kokua (helper), Ko'olau and his family had fled. The Hawaiian government in this era was controlled by a mostly American oligarchy of sugar planters, lawyers, and businessmen who had overthrown the Hawaiian Kingdom and Queen Lili'uokalani in 1893 and set up the Provisional Government that became the Republic of Hawai'i in 1895.

The first case of leprosy, known among native Hawaiians as ma'i Pake or Chinese sickness was dis-covered in Hawai'i in 1836. The disease was also called ma'i ho'oka'awale (the separating sickness) because the only way to prevent its spread was to segregate the afflicted. By the early 1870s Hansen's disease, the modern name for leprosy, was an epidemic in the Hawaiian Islands. Once diagnosed, lepers were rounded up like cattle and shipped off to the leper colony at Kalawao on Moloka'i, a peninsula cut off from the rest of the island by steep cliffs and rough seas.

Eventually the lepers were relocated to the drier Westside of the peninsula at Kalaupapa.

Exile to Kalawao often meant a death of unimaginable horror. In some cases, the afflicted would be thrown overboard and left to swim to the barren box canyon, where the "fresh" ones were often raped and robbed by gangs of lepers. Native Hawaiians referred to it as ka luakupapa'u kanu ola (the grave of living corpses). Ironically Kalauiko'olau's name translate as "the grave of Ko'olau." The work of Father Damien and others greatly improved the conditions beginning in the 1870s.

Friends and families of the lepers in hiding at Kalalau and Waimea took care of Ko'olau and his family and kept their location secret for as long as possible. Among the lepers was the once-prominent Judge Kauai, whose wife had inherited land on the Westside from King Kamehameha. The judge later became a leader of the small leper community in Kalalau. As word of these and other holdouts became known, pressure was put on the local authorities to rid the island entirely of lepers. In Waimea there were reports of conflicts between the lepers and the authorities, but generally the lepers resigned to their fate once they had been diagnosed.

Pi'ilani described at length the events of her family's exile to journalist John Sheldon who published her account in the Hawaiian language in 1906.

An English-language translation of the book by noted Hawaiian language translator Frances Frazier of Kaua'i was published by the University of Hawai'i Press in 2001 as *The True Story of Kaluaikoolau*.

Pi'ilani's lament is told in the native Hawaiian style of combining poetry and prose in storytelling, the beauty of which has not been seen since the memoirs of Queen Lili'uokalani were first released in 1898.

In her introduction to her book, Frazier refers to it as the "only factual account of a famous episode in Hawaiian history."

There are countless volumes written on Hawaiian history, but most are written from a distinctly western worldview, often reflecting neither an understanding nor an appreciation for the Hawaiian culture. Pi'ilani's perspective comes from a mother's broken heart, with a poetry and pathos that is uniquely Hawaiian.

Several other accounts of Ko'olau's life have been published, including *Ko'olau Outlaw*, by the late West Kaua'i kama'āina Valdemar Knudsen. His fictional account presents a unique personal perspective of the life and times of Ko'olau, mixing in some local history into his tale. Knudsen surreptitiously states in small print, on the back cover, under a photo of the author: "This tale may be considered a piece of historical fiction." Apparently this didn't prevent the public from assuming Knudsen's account was factual. Pi'ilani was a dear friend of the Knudsen family and referred to his grandfather as the "beloved elder Knudsen" in her memoirs.

Knudsen's account also contained a salacious subplot involving an alleged carnal interest that the local sheriff had in Ko'olau's wife. It stated: "She had the grace of a hula dancer as she walked. Her firm breasts lifted the light mumu, which then draped to her hips where the clinging material displayed the perfection of her slender body. Stolz felt his pulse quicken... when he saw Ko'olau and the girl touch their hands and walk toward the river. A hatred for this tall young Hawaiian filled his soul."

Knudsen's tale is the source of a local legend that claims Ko'olau never had leprosy, but was framed by Deputy Sheriff Stoltz in order to steal his wife. If this was true, it is unlikely that Pi'ilani would mention any of the sordid details of it in her memoirs. And if Ko'olau did not have leprosy going into Kalalau, then he must have contracted it while he was there because, according to her testimony, that is what afflicted both he and his son Kaleamanu.

Another popular misconception alluded to in *Ko'olau Outlaw* is that on the way to Moloka'i, Ko'olau jumped ship en route before hiding out in Kalalau. Again, Pi'ilani never mentions this incident in her memoirs, and states that they left for Kalalau soon after her husband was diagnosed.

Author Jack London's fictional account *Koolau the Leper* is considered the most popular of his tales set in Hawai'i. London depicts Ko'olau as a depraved, wretched soul, bent on vengeance. The Waimea deputy's son Herbert, then a student at Stanford, sailed with London aboard his yacht the *Snark* from Oakland, California, to Honolulu in 1907, and likely introduced London to Ko'olau's story.

The major difference between the two accounts is that one reads like an accident report and the other like a Shakespearean tragedy.

Pi'ilani alone knew what transpired at Waimakemake, and she cared for her husband too deeply to allow his legacy to be tarnished by sensationalism. Her work was motivated by a desire to "to tell all the true things concerning this pathetic story, so that they would understand what they had mistaken and had only guessed."

The official Provisional Government account published in government-leaning Honolulu newspapers describes a renegade leper who stood off a botched military operation, while Pi'ilani's is a tale of courage and transcendental sacrifice, which, when read in the original, would bring a reptile to tears.

This Pathetic Story—Pi'ilani and Ko'olau
By Terence Moeller

My account of the story of Pi'ilani and Ko'olau is based upon personal experiences in Kalalau Valley, upon Frances Frazier's English language translation of John Sheldon's Hawaiian language version of Pi'ilani's The True Story of Kaluai-ko'olau, *Jack London's short story "Koolau the Leper" from his Hawaiian tales book* House of Pride, *Valdemar Knudsen's* Koolau Outlaw, *and the Provisional Government Army report.*

Ko'olau and Pi'ilani were married in the town of Waimea, Kaua'i in 1881. Their first-born arrived the following year, at the same "birth sands" of his parents. The modest seventeen-year-old mother wrote in her memoirs: "The God of Gods gave them a precious gift, a beautiful son who resembled his mother." The young parents named their son Kaleimanu.

In 1889 Pi'ilani noticed a suspicious looking rash on her husband's cheeks that would come and go. She said nothing about it until Ko'olau brought it to her attention. With feigned indifference she said, "Tchah…a little redness, nothing more." They both were alarmed when Kaleimanu developed the same symptoms. As rumors of Ko'olau's condition spread in the small community, a government agent named Pokipala arrived at his door and ordered him to be examined by a doctor. Ko'olau was subsequently diagnosed as having leprosy and ordered to be confined at the Hawaiian Kingdom's leper colony at Kalawao, Moloka'i, a place known to Hawaiians as "the grave where one is buried alive."

Ko'olau was told he would have to go alone to Kalawao. Defying the ruling, the young couple who believed that no man-made law superseded the sacred bonds of marriage, made an oath to each other to remain together till parted by death.

Their family along with Pi'ilani's mother and guide set out on horseback to Kalalau Valley in the winter of 1892. Pi'ilani wrote of the ride to Kōke'e, "And in the loneliness and awesomeness of the night we turned towards the trail to climb up and descend into Kalalau." At the break of day they arrived at Halemanu Valley, stopping at the home of West Kaua'i Norwegian pioneer Valdemar Knudsen, who was known to Hawaiians as the "beloved, elder one, Kanuka." There they rested a few hours before continuing the ascent to the ridge above Kalalau Valley. When the sun rose they were standing on the heights of Kilohana (known today as the Kalalau Lookout), gazing 4,000 feet down the jagged pali.

After a tearful farewell to their companions, Pi'ilani, Ko'olau, and Kaleimanu began a perilous descent into the valley. She recalls that halfway down they were enveloped in pitch darkness and torrential rain, "on the brink of the Pali clinging on" yet they forged through to their new home.

At the time there were 148 Hawaiians living in the valley, including twenty-eight lepers. Most of the other residents of Kalalau interacted with the lepers, even sharing the same utensils without too much concern—until the victims of the disease became horribly disfigured. With old friends living in the valley, the family soon found peace and solitude in their new surroundings. Ko'olau was a sharpshooter and hunted game for the community. He was known to shoot wild goats between the ears, so as not to damage their pelt.

It was on the first day of the season of Makalapua (blossoming time) when Pi'ilani was alarmed to see Deputy Sheriff Louis "Lui" Stolz of Waimea at the mouth of the Kalalau Stream. He had descended the cliffs on an ancient Nā Pali trail known as Kalou (the hook) and was there to confront Ko'olau.

A still, small voice in Pi'ilani's heart told her, "You swore to be brave for your husband and child, therefore be brave for them." She smiled and shook the deputy sheriff's hand inviting him into their house. As they exchanged pleasantries and information about old friends, Pi'ilani noticed his eyes "darting" across the room.

When Stolz asked her about her husband, she told him truthfully that Ko'olau was working in the taro patch and invited the sheriff to wait for him to return. He pressed further about the extent of Ko'olau's illness, and Pi'ilani told him that it was about the same—the redness of his cheeks came and went. After Stolz departed, Pi'ilani recalled how overcome with grief she was that the "power of the government" had reached into this remote valley in an attempt to separate her family.

When Ko'olau returned from the taro patch, Pi'ilani told him everything. He calmly assured her that their fate was in the hands of God, and that "He would lead our footsteps on the road, which He trod for us to follow." This inspired her to write in her memoirs:

> "With me, my husband Kaluaiko'olau,
> With me, my child Kaleimanu,
> With me, you two until our bones are laid to rest,
> With me, you two until the final disappearance."

The morning had brought with it news that Stolz had commanded all lepers to be gathered on the beach at Kalalau by noon. Ko'olau and his wife were present when Stolz announced the disheartening news that all those afflicted were to secure their belongings and to be prepared to sail to the "place of leprosy" at Kalawao within a week.

Most of the lepers either consented, or said nothing. When Ko'olau arose and asked about his wife, the Sheriff replied that a kokua would not be permitted to join him. Ko'olau reminded Stolz of the sanctity of the couple's wedding vows. The sheriff took this as a challenge to his authority, and shouted that only the "sickly" would be taken to the place where they would be "cared for by the government." He parted with a final warning to the lepers at Kalalau that noncooperation would be regarded as a criminal offense.

In the days that followed, Ko'olau advised the others to keep their word, but he stated that he could not, in good conscience, leave Kalalau. Not only was he committed to protecting his son from a horrible fate, but also as a traditional Hawaiian he was also concerned about the fate of his bones upon his death, fearing they would be scattered on a distant island. He knew that if he remained in the place of his birth, his wife would hide his bones where they would not be disturbed. Furthermore, he saw that his son, whose condition had worsened, needed his mother more than ever.

Rumors of a showdown spread quickly when Stolz returned to the valley a week later. When informers reported what Ko'olau had said, Stolz responded: "Ho! You will see— Ko'olau will run for the mountains, and then he will become emaciated and have a big head. Lui Stolz will capture him, and Ko'olau will be through in Kalalau."

When Ko'olau heard this, he seemed to grow in stature and said, "Let the harm be to the one who thinks it." He clutched his rifle, which he called Kaimonakamakeloa (death afar in a wink) and swore an oath to live in peace if not disturbed, but to fight to the death to keep his family together. Pi'ilani recalled that at that moment a "great silence" fell over the valley, like the stillness before a violent storm.

Ko'olau was aware that Stolz had set up camp nearby and was waiting for an opportunity to get the drop on him. That night he and his wife were walking along the Kalalau stream toward the coast when they crossed paths with Penikila, an assistant to the sheriff, and an old friend of the couple. He asked where Stolz was. Penikila replied that he thought the sheriff had gone to Hanalei. Further on along the trail another friend contradicted Penikila, saying that Stolz was in fact waiting for Ko'olau up-valley.

The couple continued to the stream mouth where several villagers had gathered to discuss the situation. Ko'olau warned them that he had come there to face the sheriff, and that it would be better if they left. He then turned to Penikila, whom he had met on the trail, and confronted him concerning the whereabouts of Stolz. Ko'olau informed him that that if his "own thoughts were as evil as Penekila's," he would certainly be dead by now.

Rumors had circulated that the sheriff was planning to make his move as the family slept, so Ko'olau and his friend Kala stood guard throughout the evening. Meanwhile the sheriff apprehended a leper named Paoa and forced him at gunpoint to lead the way to Ko'olau's home.

As they approached the hut at around nine, Ko'olau could hear footsteps in the distance. Visibility was low, yet he had developed a keen sense of hearing.

He whispered to Pi'ilani: "Shhh...here comes the haole. Have courage, we may be going to die."

Kala was the first to spot Stolz and dashed for cover. Stolz then called out, "Kala...stand still...Stop!"

As he cocked his rifle and took aim at Kala, Ko'olau instantly rose up and shot the sheriff. The sound reverberated throughout the valley. Stolz moaned, "Hu! It hurts." Paoa pounced on the sheriff, beating him mercilessly. Ko'olau ran toward him and commanded him to stop. Stolz, who had fallen to his knees, drew his pistol. Paoa gasped, "He's going to shoot!" That instant Ko'olau fired at point blank, killing the sheriff.

The next morning a villager named Kaumeheiwa boarded his canoe and paddled to the town of Mana on the Westside to report the news of Stolz's death. Ko'olau, his family, and five other lepers retreated deep in the valley and awaited reprisal.

News of the death of Deputy Sheriff Stolz spread quickly, and a sensationalized account was reported in a Honolulu newspaper.

Sheriff Stolz Murdered by Ko'olau

"Eyewitness reports from the two deputies with Sheriff Stolz describe one of the most brutal murders ever to happen in Hawaii.

"Koolau, already a criminal from having jumped ship, refusing to go to the leper settlement at Kalaupapa, Molokai, was traced down by the indomitable efforts of Sheriff Stolz. He was located in Kalalau Valley, and the Sheriff went to force this hideous outlaw to go to Molokai. Leprosy had taken a terrible toll on the criminal's body. His left arm displayed bare bones from which his flesh hung. His face was half rotten away with the dreaded disease. When he swung his gun up to kill Stolz the gun butt rested against rotted cheeks and his exposed jawbone.

"With his dead victim before him he walked to the fallen corpse and deliberately spit his yellowish saliva into the victim's face. Such men must be found and brought to justice, or shot down like dogs. If Ko'olau outlaw escapes the reach of Hawaiian law the land will be filled with lawlessness."

A Provisional Government report states that the steamer *Waialeale* was sent to Kalalau to return Stolz's body to Waimea. A second ship, the *Iwalani*, sailed from Honolulu with thirty-five well-armed soldiers aboard. Before arriving at Kalalau, the steamer stopped at Hanalei, picking up Samuel Wilcox, his brother Luther (who served as an interpreter), and the newly sworn-in sheriff of Kaua'i.

Martial law was declared in Hanalei and Waimea, and the trails from Hanalei to Kalalau, and from Waimea to Kalalau, were closed and patrolled by police. All lepers at Kalalau were to be taken into custody within twenty-four hours. Chief Kunuiakea was also brought on board in order to gain the support of the healthy Hawaiians still residing in the valley.

The *Waialeale* then sailed to Hā'ena where it was reported that twenty of the residents of Kalalau had left the valley in fear of being arrested, though there were no lepers among them. A man from the Pa family told the captain that Ko'olau's group was hiding deep in the valley, Judge Kauai was living on the beach, and that four other lepers were also there waiting to sail to Moloka'i.

Pa agreed to guide the army into the valley, but he would not go as far as Ko'olau's home for fear of being shot. The soldiers landed on the beach at noon in calm seas, and encountered no resistance among the few lepers who met them. They immediately began a house-to-house search, where they found old Judge Kauai hiding under a bed with his hands and feet bound in dirty bandages.

Three other lepers were also apprehended in the big cave on the west end of the beach, near the falls. Guards were placed all along the stream as the soldiers established a base camp one-mile deep in the valley.

An elderly Hawaiian named Wahinealoha, who often cared for the lepers, was apprehended and ordered to find Ko'olau to tell him that if he and everyone with him did not surrender, they would be shot on sight. When Wahinealoha returned, he reported that nine lepers had consented to be taken in. Five others, including Ko'olau, remained hidden in the wilderness. The nine who agreed to surrender first demanded to speak with Chief Kunuiakea. They were guided to a private meeting place and assured by Luther Wilcox that they would remain unharmed. The following morning a scouting party consisting of fifteen soldiers, lead by Major Pratt, went deeper into the valley in search of Ko'olau and the five other holdouts.

By 4:30 p.m. the following day the lepers that had surrendered arrived in Honolulu aboard the *Waialeale*. Among those taken to the Kalihi receiving station was a seven-year-old named Ika, an eleven-year-old named Mele, and a twelve-year-old named Kio. There was a great outpouring of grief as the children were stripped from their parents' arms and forced to board a ship bound for Moloka'i. At Kalawao they would be neglected and abused, and their parents knew that this was perhaps the last time they would see them alive.

In a Provisional Government report titled *The Battle of Kalalau* published in 1893, a Captain Larson stated that he interrogated all the residents in the valley, demanding to know the whereabouts of Ko'olau and the five lepers who had joined him. Someone reported that they had gone to Hā'ena. Wahinealoha was then dispatched to Hā'ena to find out if this was true. He returned that night with a hapa-haole named Kinney, who said he thought that the five lepers had passed by his home in Hā'ena earlier in the day.

Eleven days after Stolz's death, a group of Hawaiians who resided near the beach saw Paoa and warned him: "E Paoa, return upland, as death is coming here. The *Iwalani* has landed, filled with police and soldiers armed to come and fight with Ko'olau, and there will be shooting at Kalalau until they get him dead or alive; it is not known which."

Ko'olau addressed them, reaffirming his love for his friends and his conviction that they should surrender rather than risk their lives in a battle which could never be won. He then announced to Pi'ilani that he had decided to send her and the boy away.

Pi'ilani knew in her heart that her husband was right. To remain with him meant certain death. But she believed a vow could never be broken, and so she declared she would stay. She swore to die an "evil death" if ever she did not fulfill her pledge to sacrifice her life for her family. Because of this oath, Ko'olau was honor-bound to allow Pi'ilani to remain.

Ko'olau and Pi'ilani bid farewell to their friends and they immersed themselves in the "awesome wilderness of Kalalau." There they made a refuge high above the stream at Waimakemake Falls. Sheer cliffs were at their backs, a steep incline was before them, and dense vegetation covered either side. Their feet dangled in the air as they shared a family meal of poi and dried squid. There, for a time, they felt safe and the inspired young wahine penned another verse:

"Within the seconds, the minutes, and the hours,
Within the loneliness and sorrow
Within the flowers, the leaves and everything,
Within you and without, I am with you."

Pi'ilani recalled: "Then we were startled to hear shouting below and we realized that we had been guarded by the Holy Spirit. We heard and understood without mistake that from the voices of the haoles and the sound of their arms, this was an army...You should know how filled with terror I was...but I fended it off with bravery and the determination to be fearless. I understood with inner chill and alarm that we were face to face with death."

From their vantage point they began to see that the government troops had left a trail of destruction in their wake. Paoa's home and those of several of their friends were burned in the village below. This infuriated Pi'ilani more than anything:

"This was the wickedness and worthlessness of these impertinent P.G. soldier's actions toward the blameless ones and their houses and their belongings... My husband and I were filled with rage, and if perhaps we could have gotten some of them we would have wrung their bones and fed them to the fire. Until this day I am not done brooding over these plundering, burning, thieving kolea, the birds who come to fatten on our land, who come as wanderers and arrogantly lived off the sweet breast of our native land!"

The Provisional Government soldiers set up fortifications below Ko'olau's position. Then suddenly they opened fire.

Pi'ilani panicked, but her husband's calm inspired bravery in her. Soon "fear had disappeared." In the face of certain death she embraced her child and waited for the end. Suddenly a soldier garbed in red woolen long johns appeared not far from where they were sitting. In the wink of an eye, Ko'olau shot him.

At the sight of their fallen comrade, the remaining soldiers fled down the steep terrain and took up defensive positions. In the fierce counterattack that followed, Pi'ilani recalled that the bullets struck everywhere around them "except where we sat." She wrote that there came a point in the siege that the bullets striking around them "seemed as nothing."

The nonstop assault continued well into the night, and began at dawn, the air so thick with smoke that it was difficult to breathe. That morning Ko'olau told Piilani and Kaleimanu to put on new garments in order to be "properly dressed for death." It was agreed that when the end came they would take their own lives, "to avoid harm at the hands of the bloody soldiers."

Though they were close to a waterfall they had run out of water, unable to expose themselves. To quench their thirst, Pi'ilani tediously gathered the morning dew off leaves.

Voices of soldiers could be heard clearly as they moved in for a final assault. A group of them climbed to an elevation just above the holdout and were preparing to shoot down on the family when Ko'olau spotted one of them peering through the jungle and shot him. As the wounded man rolled down an embankment, another soldier scrambling for cover in a panic accidentally shot himself. The others retreated down the cliffs.

The assault continued four days. So many bullets had been shot in their direction that there was "scarcely any vegetation" left on the trees. Ko'olau wept at seeing Kaleimanu suffer from hunger and thirst. He told Pi'ilani that in the evening they must steal away under the cover of darkness. This was most difficult for the child, whose fingers were paralyzed and whose feet were covered with infected sores, yet he never complained. As they slowly descended from their holdout they could hear the talk of soldiers all about them. At the stream they quenched their thirst and with extreme difficulty crossed to the other side.

After spending the night at a friend's house, they ascended the side of the valley to a secret place in the heights of Limamuku, above Waimakemake waterfall. There they were comfortable and nourished themselves with freshwater prawns, bananas, and taro. As they rested and regained their strength, they were suddenly awakened by the sound of a cannon blast echoing throughout the valley. Several more shots followed and they could see that Waimakemake was being bombarded. They counted a total of 19 Howitzer shells fired at their former hideout.

Pi'ilani built a fire that night and cooked freshwater 'o'opu. After a week at Limamuku, Pi'ilani reported that they no longer heard the sound of gunfire and presumed that the soldiers had returned home, and given them up for dead. She wondered, "Who could escape?"

The Provisional Government wasn't taking any chances. Their report states:

"The steamship, *Iwalani*, left Honolulu at four o'clock Monday evening and arrived quickly at the battle site of Kalalau with ten more soldiers under Corporal King, with more food and arms, such as shells, cannonballs and dynamite. Also sent were three containers for the bodies of the three soldiers who died at Kalalau. On this expedition was Atty. General Smith with new boots for the troops."

Ko'olau and Pi'ilani lived at Limamaku for a month without being detected by the troops. Ko'olau constantly scouted the area, never letting his guard down. When he felt confident that it was safe, they moved down to a lower elevation along the stream called Oheoheiki. In the daytime they would return to the cliffs, and at night they would camp along the stream, where food was more abundant.

For two years they lived in a way that Pi'ilani described as a "period of dreamy loneliness." Often they would see friends, but their friends could not see them. She wrote that there was "no lack of conjecture of what had happened to them," but most assumed that the soldiers had killed them.

One day Pi'ilani (who had been wearing her husband's coat and hat at the time), was pulling some taro along the stream when the hapa-haole, Kinney, and two Hawaiians saw her. They mistook her for a thief and hollered at her. Pi'ilani quickly ran home to tell her husband, and when she arrived, the three men, who had followed her, approached the camp. They were amazed to discover that it was their old friends, and they were overcome with joy.

Hearing news about friends and family comforted Pi'ilani, who suffered most from loneliness. She said, "We seemed as persons who had died and come to life again." As they bid farewell, Kinney said, "Eh, listen, if you see a steer and you know it is mine, take it for yourself, I give it to you." Ko'olau had many opportunities to accept this generous offer, yet as much as he longed for the taste of beef, he would never take what he knew he could not repay.

The following day two more dear friends met them and they "wailed together in their greeting." The couple returned with gifts of food, clothing, and supplies, which were sorely needed.

Ko'olau, his wife, and son spent the next three-and-a-half years wandering in the valley, never spending more than two or three days in the same place. During that time many of their friends searched for them, wanting to help them, but they remained hidden in the "deep gloom of the mountain forest."

There had been attempts to follow their tracks, but Pi'ilani wrote that they never got a glimpse of them because they were "hidden and cloaked in secrecy by the alert one of the Kalalau cliffs, the brave one who singly had routed the soldiers of the Provisional Government...And he lived as an ali'i on the famous heights of Kamaile, from whence the fire was flung."

It is not clear whether Ko'olau's self-imposed exile, long after the battle with the government army was over, resulted from his fear of capture, or because his appearance had deteriorated to the point that he no longer could bear to be seen by his loved ones.

The Provisional Government report never acknowledged that Ko'olau had survived, only that "his body was never recovered." Nor was there ever an acknowledgement of wrongdoing in regard to the burning of the homes of Kalalau residents. With this being the only source of information to the public, the gap between fact and revisionism grew, and the deeds and motivations of the fugitive family were lost. E uhi ana ka wa i hala i na mea i hala (passing time obscures the past).

After years of wandering in the wilderness Kaleimanu's condition deteriorated, and he constantly cried from the pain in his stomach. Pi'ilani tried treating him with herbs, which temporarily alleviated the pain, but she knew the end was near. On the day of his death, Kaleimanu placed his arms around his mother's neck and whispered, "Where is papa? I am going to sleep." She knew what this meant, and wept inconsolably. As Ko'olau rushed to his side and caressed his son, the boy smiled slightly, and then drew his final breath.

Pi'ilani recalls that for another year they stayed deep in the wilderness mourning the loss of Kaleimanu. Although they often saw their friends in the valley, they remained hidden from them and had no one else to share their grief. Ko'olau began to develop the same symptoms in his stomach, and sensed his time was near. He told Pi'ilani that when he died, she should end her exile. "Tell the truth if you are questioned, saying that mine was the trouble and that you fulfilled an oath that you swore."

Soon Ko'olau slipped into a coma. Pi'ilani wrote: "And in the middle of the night, during the turning of the Milky Way, the light in the house that was Kaluaiko'olau was extinguished, and his spirit returned to the One who made him, leaving only his clay behind for me to lament over—I alone in the awesome loneliness which was peopled only with the voices of the land shells, which seemed to lament with me in those hours before the break of dawn."

She found a place at Waimakemake Falls sheltered by the cliffs and concealed in the tangled palai ferns and gingers. It was there that she dug her husband's grave. A lei of lehua and ferns was placed upon his breast and, in keeping with his last request, his rifle Kaimonakamakeloa was placed in his hand.

She had only a knife with which to dig his grave, but Pi'ilani was determined to bury him properly, so that no "abuse" would come to his bones. After the first day had passed, only half of the depth was finished. That night she slept beside the body of her husband and completed the grim task at dawn. She planted slips from the forest around his grave, "kissed the earth, and left him there sleeping the sleep of seasons."

In her lament, Pi'ilani wrote:

"Remembrance at facing death together from the bullets of the soldiers of the Provisional Government which had flown everywhere, remembrance of the banks of the irrigated taro terraces, the valleys, the steep ridges, where we had gone together—auwe, the aching pain of grief—auwe, my husband and my child—auwe, I groan with love of them—seeking to be soothed, but no, they are hidden away, they have left me forever—it is for me to feel the pangs—auwe, auwe, auwe."

Pi'ilani did not return home but made her "nest in a Kalalau thorn thicket" where she mourned for months.

> "And when the last trumpet
> sounds the mighty earth shall shake
> And death shall yield his ancient sword
> And dust to life awake
> And those asleep in Christ shall rise,
> immortal as the spring
> Oh grave where is thy victory now?
> And where, oh death, thy sting?"

She remained vigilant and in complete solitude, surviving off the taro and freshwater shellfish. Pi'ilani longed to return to her loved ones, but feared that if the government learned of her whereabouts, she would be arrested. Finally, the day came when Pi'ilani would make the long journey home to Kekaha. She returned the same way she came, on the ancient Kalou trail, "looking for the resting place on the Ascent of Kilohana." As dawn broke, she recalls stepping on the high peak of the pali of Kalou where "every glance reveals death," and there is no place to go but straight up.

She climbed until nightfall and turning back she saw the lights of the houses in Kalalau twinkling in the distance, stirring deep emotions that became a chant: "Oh the succoring hospitable valley of Kalalau...You will be hidden from my sight, but always in my heart."

Pi'ilani didn't encounter another person along the way home, and when she arrived at her mother-in-law's house in Kekaha there was great wailing at the news of the deaths of Ko'olau and Kaleimanu. The legend of Ko'olau had already reached the Neighbor Islands and the news of the return of his faithful wife soon became widespread. Within days the new sheriff of Kaua'i had come to Piilani's residence in Kekaha to speak with her. She told him the whole truth and in the end was absolved of any wrongdoing.

The strength of her aloha, discovered in the crucible of her suffering, sustained Pi'ilani and inspired her to immortalize Ko'olau in her writings. The poet remained at her "birth sands" for the rest of her life, comforted by the thought that one day she would see her beloved Ko'olau and Kaleimanu again.

GLOSSARY

'a'a	Sharp lava rocks
'āina	The land
ahupua'a	Valley land division extending from the uplands to the sea
akamai	Smart
aloha	Love, to love, mercy, compassion, greetings, goodbye
Apple of Sodom	Poisonous fruit growing on Kalalau Beach which resembles a tomato
Back door	Trails that take the back way into Kalalau Valley
Big Cave	The largest grotto on the west end of Kalalau Beach
Big Pool	Popular swimming hole in Kalalau
Bobo's rock	A large rock on the west end of Kalalau Beach where Bobo likes to fish
brother	Also known as bro, bra, brudda, blala, co-bro, or cuz
camper	Spends the first night at Hanakoa, carries tent stakes and sterno and has permits
choke	Plenty of
cleansing	Anything from a sweat lodge to a hurricane
da-kine	Anything you want it to be
derby	Cockfight
'e'epa	Supernatural beings of the forest, common in Hawaiian myths and legends.
Ginger Pool	Gentle waterfall in Kalalau that fills a pool laced with ginger
hapa-haole	Part haole
happening	In season or ripe
Hawaiian Way	Living off the 'āina
he'e	Octopus also known as tako
heiau	A Hawaiian place of worship constructed prior to 1820

Honeymoon Suite	Campsite on Kalalau Beach between the river and Milo Forest
Ho'ole Falls	Waterfall at the west end of Kalalau Beach
Hunting license	A season pass into Kalalau
ika	Squid
imu	Cooking pit
Java Plum Forest	Campsite on Kalalau Beach
kama'āina	Traditionally means "native born" though often referred to as non-native born haoles who have lived in Hawai'i a long time.
kapu	Taboo
kahuna	Hawaiian priest
Kalalau stew	A combination of everything that makes it into the pot for dinner
Kaumuali'i	Last reigning King of Kaua'i
konani board	Hawaiian checker board
kuleana	Hawaiian's homestead, responsibility
kumu	Teacher
kumu hula	Teacher of hula
lava lava	Cloth wrap
liliko'i	A yellow or purple delicacy known as passion fruit.
makai	Toward the ocean
mauka	Toward the mountains
malihini	Newcomer to the islands
mana	Spiritual power
Menehune	The legendary first inhabitants of Kaua'i
manahune	Tahitain word for Menehune, and commoners
Milo Forest	Camping area on Kalalau Beach
mo'o	Supernatural reptile-like creature common in Hawaiian myths and legends
mountain apple	Succulent red fruit found on the Nā Pali trail

Night Marchers	Deceased Hawaiian ancestors who march the trails at night
naupaka	A native species of mountain or seashore flower which forms a half-blossom
'ohana	Family
okole	Butt
'o'opu	A delicious native Hawaiian freshwater fish plentiful in Kalalau streams.
'ōpae	Freshwater shrimp
outlaw	Nonpermit-holding resident of Kalalau
Outlaw Pool	A swimming hole in Kalalau
pali	Sea cliff
puka	Hole
Red Hill	Last ridge which descends into Kalalau Valley
red-tailed tropic bird	Rare white seabird with one-foot-long red tail feathers seen in Kalalau.
Riverside Café	A former gathering place along the Kalalau Stream
Space Rock	A giant boulder at the highest point of the Nā Pali trail with a spectacular view
Smoke Rock	A large clearing in the center of the valley with a large boulder and a panoramic view
talk story	Local dialogue
tabis	Japanese-style reef walkers sometimes used on the trail
Tom's Garden	A two-acre orchard in Kalalau Valley, established by Kalalau Tom
umu	oven
Waimakemake	The falls where Ko'olau and his family hid
yahoo sticks	Sticks that the Rainbow Rabbi juggles

BIBLIOGRAPHY

Barrére, Dorothy; Mary Kawena Pukui, Marion Kelly, *Hula: Historical Perspectives Pacific Anthropological Records Number 30*, Honolulu: Bishop Museum Press, 1980.

Bell, Graham V., *Kaua'i's Nā Pali Coast—A Unique Adventure*, Unique Adventure Press, 1990.

Bennett, Wendell, *Archaeology of Kauai*, Bishop Museum Bulletin 80, Honolulu: Bishop Museum Press, 1931.

Bingham, Hiram, *A Residence of Twenty-One Years in the Sandwich Islands*, Privately printed, 1847.

Clark, John R.K., *Beaches of Kaua'i and Ni'ihau*, University of Hawai'i Press, 1990.

Day, A. Grove, *The Hawaiian Reader—A Collection of Stories*, Mutual Publishing, 1984.

Emory, Tiare, *Hawaiian Life in Kalalau, Kauai according to John Hanohano and his mother, Wahine-i-Keouli Pa*, Manuscript, Bishop Museum, 1949.

Fairechild, Diana, *Noni*, Flyana Rhyme, 1998.

Frazier, Frances, "Battle of Kalalau" as Reported in the Newspaper Kuokoa, *Hawaiian Journal of History*, Vol. 23, 1989.

Frazier, Frances, *The True Story of Kaluaikoolau As Told by His Wife, Piilani*, University of Hawai'i Press, 2001.

Handy, E.S. Craighill and Elizabeth Green Handy with Mary Kawena Pukui, *Native Planters in Old Hawai'i—Their Life, Lore, and Environment*, Bishop Museum Bulletin 233, Bishop Museum Press, 1972.

Joesting, Edward, *Kaua'i—The Separate Kingdom*, University of Hawai'i Press, 1984.

Kirch, Patrick, *Feathered Gods and Fishhooks—An Introduction to Hawaiian Archaeology and Prehistory*, University of Hawai'i Press, 1985.

Knudsen, Valdemar, *Koolau, Outlaw*, Privately published, 1976.

London, Jack, *The House of Pride and other Tales of Hawaii*, Macmillian, 1911.

Merwin, W.S., *The Folding Cliffs*, Alfred A. Knopf, 1998.

Peebles, Douglas and Chris Cook, *From The Skies of Paradise—Kaua'i*, Mutual Publishing, 1991.

Pukui, Mary Kawena, *'Olelo No'eau—Hawaiian Proverbs and Poetical Sayings*, Honolulu: Bishop Museum Press, 1983.

Ressencourt, Eugene, "Oahu Man Repeats Kalalau Climb With Two Friends," *The Garden Island* newspaper, September 12, 1962.

Smith, Robert, *Hiking Kauai: The Garden Isle*, Wilderness Press, 1977.

Summers, Catherine C., *The Hawaiian Grass House in Bishop Museum Special Publication 80*, Honolulu: Bishop Museum 1988.

TenBruggencate, Jan, "The Hermit of Kalalau dead at 72," *The Honolulu Advertiser*, December 1991.

Valier, Kathy, *On the Nā Pali Coast—A Guide for Hikers and Boaters*, Honolulu: University of Hawai'i Press, 1988.

Vancouver, George, *Voyage of Discovery to the North Pacific Ocean and Round the World*, Da Capo Press, 1968.

Wichman, Fredrick, *Kaua'i: Ancient Place-Names and Their Stories*, Honolulu: University of Hawai'i Press, 2001.

ABOUT THE AUTHORS

Terence James Moeller hails from Texas, and at the age of 15 adopted Hawai'i as his home. After living in the jungle in Kealakekua, Kona, for a year in the early '70s, he moved to the infamous Waimānalo Beach and commuted to Windward Community College in Kāne'ohe. Having survived that experience, he transferred to S.F.A.S.U. earning an undergraduate degree in Communications and a master's degree in Interdisciplinary Studies in the school of fine arts. For the last two decades he has been an independent producer on Kaua'i, creating historical documentaries, stringing for the four Honolulu TV news stations, and doing freelance photo journalism.

His interest in film led to the writing of several screenplays, and working on film crews, including all three *Jurassic Park* films, which were shot on location on the Garden Isle. He recently finished a children's book, which will be published under his own label. As a companion piece to *Dramas of Kalalau*, he has also produced a documentary video entitled *Inside Kalalau*.

William Gladstone is one of the country's top literary agents and media experts. In 1982, he founded his own agency, publishing, and film company, Waterside Productions Inc. in Cardiff, California where he still lives. Best known for representing the creators of the "For Dummies...." book series and individual authors ranging from Eckhart Tolle to Dick Wolf, Gladstone spends a great deal of time on Kaua'i and whenever he can in the Kalalau Valley. He is a director of the Club of Budapest, a philanthropic European based organization dedicated to raising planetary awareness. He has traveled extensively all over the world and concurs with the Dalai Lama that the Kalalau Valley is one of the most sacred and mystical locations on earth.